# MICHAEL HOLST
## 53.627 WORTE | 53,627 WORDS

Michael Holst

# 53.627 WORTE | 53,627 WORDS

Interviews und Statements | Interviews and Statements

Mit Beiträgen von
Hans Peter Markstein und Yoko Kawakami
Herausgegeben von Marcellus M. Menke

With Contributions from
Hans Peter Markstein and Yoko Kawakami.
Edited by Marcellus M. Menke

# Edition HIC<

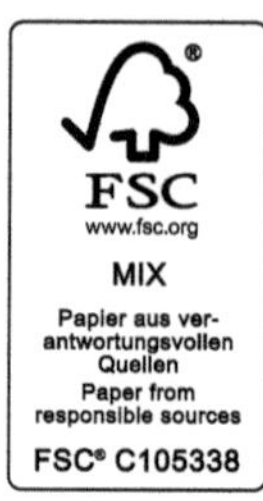

Michael Holst: 53.627 WORTE | 53,627 WORDS
Interviews und Statements | Interviews and Statements

Mit Beiträgen von Hans Peter Markstein und Yoko Kawakami.
Herausgegeben von Marcellus M. Menke | With Contributions from Hans
Peter Markstein and Yoko Kawakami. Edited by Marcellus M. Menke

Edition HIC<, Köln 2025

Satz: m4-Systems Cologne

Covergestaltung: Marcellus M. Menke unter Verwendung eines Ausschnitts
aus Michael Holst: „No dystopia at all, believe in the future!" Acryl auf
Karton 75 x 98 cm, Werkverzeichnis MH2024-07-12-KHL-4416-mr-
w185ge2 | Cover design: Marcellus M. Menke using an excerpt from Michael
Holst: "No dystopia alt all, believe in the future!" acrylic on cardboard 75 x
98 cm, catalog raisonné MH2024-07-12-KHL-4416-mr-w185ge2

Bibliografische Information der Deutschen Nationalbibliothek: Die
Deutsche Nationalbibliothek verzeichnet diese Publikation in der Deutschen
Nationalbibliografie; detaillierte bibliografische Daten sind im Internet über
dnb.dnb.de abrufbar. | Bibliographic information of the German National
Library: The German National Library lists this publication in the Deutsche
Nationalbibliografie; Detailed bibliographic data is available on the Internet
via dnb.dnb.de.



Verlag: BoD · Books on Demand GmbH, Überseering 33, 22297 Hamburg,
bod@bod.de
Druck: Libri Plureos GmbH, Friedensallee 273, 22763 Hamburg

ISBN: 978-3-8192-2981-7

# Inhalt | Contents

# Ein Künstler im Gespräch

*Eine Einführung von Marcellus M. Menke*

Michael Holst ist es immer wichtig gewesen im Gespräch zu bleiben, im Gespräch mit den Menschen die seine Kunst rezipieren, den Besuchern seiner Ausstellungen und Installationen, den Menschen die sich in einer Galerie oder auf einer der vielen digitalen Plattformen seine Werke anschauen. Ich selbst habe ihn in Frankfurt bei einer seiner ganz frühen Aktions-Installationen seines Goethe Projektes kennengelernt: offen und konzentriert, mit großem Ernst und spielerischer Leichtigkeit, immer darauf bedacht, dass der Fokus des Publikums mehr auf das Thema seiner Installation, die Aussage seiner Werke, als auf seine Person geht. Michael Holst nutzt die Präsenz, die er mit seiner künstlerischen Persönlichkeit intuitiv entfaltet, zur Sensibilisierung, zur Aktivierung von Wahrnehmungsfähigkeit und Rezeptionsbereitschaft.

Dabei schlüpft Michael Holst in viele Rollen und Figuren. Er wird Teil des künstlerischen Projektes, wechselt zwischen der Rolle des Schaffenden und der des Geschaffenen. In dieser Vielfalt ist er zu allererst ganz und vollständig Schöpfer. Er schafft Ideen und Konstellationen, gestaltet Farbe und Formen, Prozesse in Raum und Zeit. Gleichzeitig schaut er mit unbefangener Neugierde als überrascht affizierter Beobachter auf das was er geschaffen hat, und was im Prozess des Schauens noch einmal, oder vielleicht erst da wirklich fassbar, entsteht. So intensiv und präsent wie er in der Rolle des kreativ Erzeugenden ist, so intensiv und präsent ist er auch der aufmerksam Zuhörende, der Zuschauer, ein Hinzu-Schauender, der aufnimmt, reflektiert, wahrnimmt der hin-zu-kommt zu dem Kunstwerk, der mit seinem Schauen ein Teil des Werkes wird.

Und das wünscht er sich auch von und für die Menschen, die seine Werke sehen, die seine Installationen und Aktionen besuchen. Teilhabe und Teilwerden.

Das erklärt warum Michael Holst der Kontakt, der Austausch, das Teilen von Erfahrung mit seinem Publikum so wichtig ist. Dieser kleine Band, in dem Interviewäußerungen und Statements der letzten 25 Jahre zusammengestellt sind, entstand aus dem Bestreben diesem Kontakt mit dem Publikum einen gesammelten Ort zu geben. Ein Rückblick, eine Bestandsaufnahme, auch ein Ort des Überblicks und der Orientierung. Die meisten Texte dieses Bandes stammen aus Zeitschriften und Ausstellungskatalogen. Doch auch Neues findet sich in der Zusammenstellung: ein ganz aktuelles Interview, das Sandra Farinelli mit dem Künstler aus Anlass seiner jüngsten Ausstellung führte und das hier zum ersten Mal abgedruckt wird.

Die Zusammenstellung dieses Bandes bietet den Blick auf mehr als 25 Jahre künstlerischen Schaffens. Sie beginnt, typisch für Michael Holst, mit der Gegenwart. Die neuen Waschbeckenbilder zeichnen die Spur, die dieser Künstler immer wieder neu für sein Publikum legen will, um es möglich zu machen, zwischen Vergangenem und Zukunft über die Brücke der Gegenwart zum Verständnis von Sein und Seiendem zu kommen.

*[Rom, im April 2025]*

# An Artist in Dialogs

*An introduction by Marcellus M. Menke*

It has always been important to Michael Holst to remain in dialog with the people who receive his art, the visitors to his exhibitions and installations, the people who view his works in a gallery or on one of the many digital platforms. I myself got to know Michael Holst in Frankfurt at one of his very early action installations of his Goethe Project: open and concentrated, with great seriousness and playful lightness, always making sure that the focus of the audience is more on the theme of his installation, the message of his works, than on his person. Michael Holst uses the presence that he intuitively unfolds with his artistic personality to sensitize, to activate the ability to perceive and the willingness to receive.

In doing so, Michael Holst slips into many roles and figures. He becomes part of the artistic project, alternating between the role of the creator and that of the created. In this multitudinousness, firstly he is foremost fully and completely the creator. He creates ideas and constellations, shapes color and form, processes in space and time. At the same time, he looks at what he has created with unbiased curiosity as a surprised observer, and what emerges once again in the process of looking, or perhaps only then becomes truly tangible. As intense and present as he is in the role of the creative producer, he is intense and present as the attentive listener, the spectator, the onlooker who takes in, reflects, perceives, who comes to the work of art, who becomes a part of this work with his looking.

And that is also what he wants from and for the people who see his works, who visit his installations and actions. Participation and becoming part of it.

This explains why contact, exchange and sharing experiences with his audience is so important to Michael Holst. This small volume, in which interviews and statements from the last 25 years have been compiled, is the result of an effort to give this contact with the public a collective place. A retrospective, a stocktaking, also a place of overview and orientation. Most of the texts in this volume are taken from magazines and exhibition catalogs. But there is also something new in the compilation: a very recent interview that Sandra Farinelli conducted with the artist on the occasion of his most recent exhibition. This interview is printed here for the first time.

The compilation of this volume offers a view of more than 25 years of artistic work. Typical for Michael Holst, it begins with the present. The new washbasin pictures trace the trail that this artist always wants to lay anew for his audience in order to make it possible to come to an understanding of being and existence between the past and the future via the bridge of the present.

*[Rome, April 2025]*

# Neue Waschbeckenbilder

*Die deutsch-italienische Journalistin Sandra Farinelli im Gespräch mit Michael Host anlässlich der Eröffnung der Ausstellung „Einige neue Bilder meines Waschbeckens"*

*Sandra Farinelli:* Ganz herzlich willkommen hier im Art-Forum 72. Ich freue mich, dass Sie sich die Zeit für dieses Gespräch nehmen. Wir sitzen im Hauptsaal Ihrer neuen Ausstellung und im Hintergrund hängt eines dieser überdimensional großen Bilder. Ich glaube es ist der größte Abzug hier in der Installation, zwei Meter Achtzig mal drei Meter neunzig, wenn ich das auf der kleinen Infotafel neben dem Bild richtig gesehen habe. Deshalb meine erste Frage ganz einfach: Ist Größe für Sie ein Thema?

*Michael Holst:* Nun, es geht um Räume und wenn man eine Ausstellung macht, dann geht es um Wirkung. Und da müssen die Bilder, die man hängt auch passen, in ihrer Größe, zu dem Raum und zu den Menschen die sie sehen. Das ist für mich auch immer sehr wichtig, die Frage wo steht jemand der auf ein Bild schaut. Wie ist das wenn man einen Raum betritt, wie ist das wenn man durch den Raum geht. Das ist, selbst wenn es eine Ausstellung ist, in der ‚nur' Bilder an der Wand oder im Raum hängen, eine wichtige Frage. Eigentlich ist das genau wie bei einer Installation, wenn man mit Objekten im Raum ein Erlebnis inszeniert. Das ist auch bei der Präsentation von Photographie so. Und da ist es natürlich klasse, gerade bei Photographie, dass man da einfach Abzüge, oder Inkprints, das sind das ja hier, gerade die großen Bilder Inkprints, in wirklich praktisch allen Größen und auf sehr vielen unterschiedlichen Materialien machen kann. Und dann kann ich einem Besucher auch dieses riesengroße Bild in einer Dimension anbieten, die in seine Wohnung oder in seinem Büro passt. Ich mache ja auch Büroausstattungen oder Empfangshallen für Unternehmen, und da sind die Anforderungen an das Format einfach sehr unterschiedlich, ganz ohne Wertung, einfach funktional. Es muss passen. Und ja, deshalb Größe ist wichtig, aber Größe heißt eben einfach nicht nur riesengroße sondern Größe heißt, die richtige Größe, die für den Raum passende Größe und das hier sind eben sehr große Räume und da müssen es dann auch sehr große Prints sein.

*Sandra Farinelli:* Und dann das Waschbecken. Es sind ja alles Bilder eines Waschbeckens. Mein Gedanke war, so schon nach einigen Minuten eigentlich, als ich so, da war noch nicht alles ganz aufgebaut, aber es hingen schon alle Bilder, und ich ging da alleine, und noch ohne die Kommentare die da jetzt neben den Bildern an der Wand oder auf einem Aufsteller stehen, und da war meine Frage: Was ist das für ein Waschbecken? Heute fragt man ja auch immer ob die Bilder echte Fotografien sind, oder von KI generiert und Sie haben ja auch gerade ein Projekt gemacht in dem Sie, zusammen mit dieser japanischen Programmiererin ...

*Michael Holst:* ... ja, mit Aiko Ito ...

*Sandra Farinelli:* ... ja genau, dieses Projekt mit den durch Computerprozesse erzeugten Bildern gemacht haben.

Michael Holst: Sie meinen „the invisible"

*Sandra Farinelli:* Ja. Und da einfach wirklich diese Frage: Was ist das für ein Waschbecken? Ist das ein echtes

Waschbecken, eines das Sie benutzen, morgens zum Rasieren zum Beispiel? Sie sind heute sehr gut rasiert, habe ich den Eindruck. Sie tragen ja sonst auch schon mal Bart.

*Michael Holst:* Danke *(lächelt).*

*Sandra Farinelli:* Also gibt es das wirklich, dieses Waschbecken. Ist das bei Ihnen zu Hause. Oder haben Sie das gefunden auf einer Deponie? Oder ...

*Michael Holst:* ... also mit der Deponie, das überrascht mich jetzt, und zu Hause, das ist so etwas was mir wichtig ist, die Privatsphäre auch zu schützen. Obwohl ich ja bei meinen Installationen und Aktionen auch immer sehr persönlich bin, aber eben nicht privat.

*Sandra Farinelli:* Aber durch den Titel mit dem Possessivpronomen da suggerieren Sie das ja doch auch schon. Oder?

*Michael Holst:* Also ja, klar. Aber gleichzeitig habe ich mir vorgenommen da nicht mehr zu sagen als die Bilder zeigen, oder vielleicht präziser noch, eigentlich nichts zu sagen, dazu und zu solchen Fragen und die Bilder sprechen zu lassen. Und wenn man sich so auf diese Bilder einlässt, und auch auf den Titel und was es hier in der Ausstellung an Texten dazu gibt, dann kann das gut wirken und ist dann vielleicht auch eine Antwort auf Ihre Frage. Und ja, klar es ist mein Waschbecken. Ich bin der Besitzer. Wir haben bei den großen Projekten im Team ja auch immer einen Juristen dabei. Das ist ja wichtig und die Juristen unterscheiden immer zwischen Besitzer und Eigentümer. – So viel habe ich da schon gelernt. – Der Besitzer bin, wie gesagt, ich. Der Eigentümer ist mein Vermieter. Ich habe das Atelier ja gemietet. Und deshalb kann ich dieses Waschbecken auch nicht verkaufen, so einfach.

*Sandra Farinelli:* Hätten Sie es denn verkaufen können? Gab es da Interessenten?

*Michael Holst:* Witzigerweise ja. Man könnte das natürlich abbauen. Aber das geht so natürlich nicht, rechtlich. Da müsste ich den Vermieter fragen, also den Eigentümer *(lacht).* Also es ist das Waschbecken im Atelier in Köln. Das Atelier, das Marcellus für mich gefunden hat, und da ist so ein Waschbecken, aus den 1970er Jahren, in dem kleinen abgetrennten Raum, und das habe ich gesehen und dann war es ein Objekt, und eigentlich nur selten benutzt, aber mit einer Entwicklung. Und das ist eigentlich alles was ich dazu sagen kann. Das geht ja auch um Zeit um Spuren von Zeit, das ist so ein Thema das da drin liegt.

*Sandra Farinelli:* Ich habe gelesen, dass Sie gesagt haben, dass diese Bilder Anti-Kriegsbilder sind. Wie meinen Sie das?

*Michael Holst:* Ich glaube das ist aus einem Interview, das Zitat, dass Sie da im Kopf haben, aus einem Interview mit einer der beiden großen Frankfurter Zeitungen. Ich denke da haben Sie dieses Zitat gelesen. Die haben das da etwas überspitzt wiedergegeben, oder pointiert, könnte man auch sagen. So wie das schon mal passiert, bei Journalisten, die etwas auf den Punkt bringen wollen. Also wörtlich, so ganz direkt, eins zu eins, ist das nicht von mir. Obwohl das inhaltlich, wenn man das richtig versteht, natürlich völlig zutreffend ist.

*Sandra Farinelli:* Das müssen Sie erklären, denke ich.

*Michael Holst:* Nun, ich habe gesagt, dass diese Bilder und diese Ausstellung ein Statement gegen den Krieg sind und zwar auf eine sehr grundsätzliche Art. Sie sind gegen das Krieg-Machen und -Planen und -Rechtfertigen und -Vorbereiten und auch ein pointiertes Statement gegen die Art, wie dann später mit all den Verbrechen und den grauseligen Fürchterlichkeiten umgegangen wird, die da alle im Krieg gemacht werden, und die das Wesen des Krieges sind.

*Sandra Farinelli:* Wie stellen Sie da den Zusammenhang her? Ihre Bilder – Bilder eines Waschbeckens – und Krieg?

*Michael Holst:* Es ist natürlich ein Beuys-Thema, diese Sache mit dem Waschbecken. Das war ja schon im ersten Projekt, bei den 72 Bilder, auch im Untertitel, schon, so. Und hier ist es noch einmal aufgenommen, ganz aktuell. Das ist ja ein Thema, Krieg, ‚wieder‘, könnte man sagen. Bei uns hier in Europa ist das ‚wieder‘ richtig. Weltweit betrachtet waren da immer Kriege, größere und kleinere, und die meisten vergessen im Bewusstsein der Weltöffentlichkeit. Ja und wie wir heute, jetzt, hier, darüber reden, denken, das ist doch, finde ich, erschreckend. Und das steht irgendwie auf ganz schmerzliche Weise dem entgegen, wie wir in der Aufarbeitung oder den Versuchen der Aufarbeitung von Krieg hier in Europa bisher darüber geredet haben, besonders in Deutschland natürlich. Da habe ich immer diese ‚nie wieder‘ im Ohr. Und ich glaube das war sehr ernst gemeint. Aber das ist mit einmal, so ganz plötzlich, verklungen, verhallt im leeren Raum eines Universums, das andere Koordinaten bekommen hat, in dem mit anderen Längeneinheiten gemessen wird, sehr disruptiv. Und dieser Versuch eine Gesellschaft, einen Kontinent, vielleicht ja sogar die Welt, davor zu schützen, dass Menschen in Massen wieder bestialisch aufeinander einschlagen, sich verletzen, sich gegenseitig mit Sprengstoff und hoch beschleunigten scharfkantigen Metallgegenständen bewerfen, dieser Versuch, so ernsthaft er unternommen war, der ist gescheiter, muss man wohl sagen und das bereits bei der allerersten Belastung. *(Holt Luft)* Wir bereiten wieder Krieg vor, betrieben ihn. Und das „wir" ist hier ganz weit gefasst gemeint: Wir Menschen. Dabei war man doch so erschüttert, nach all den Grausamkeiten und Verbrechen, nach zwei Weltkriegen. Und Krieg ist immer ein Verbrechen und er führt dazu, dass auch die Unschuldigen, die Opfer, in Situationen kommen, wo sie denken – ich sage das ganz ohne Wertung, ich weiß nicht ob das von einem moralischen Standpunkt richtig oder falsch ist – dass sie, das praktisch ein jeder, denkt etwas tun zu müssen, was er normalerweise als ethisch verboten ansieht. Das sind wirklich richtig grundsätzliche Fragen. Und natürlich leben sich da die Menschen aus, die, aus was für Gründen auch immer, eine Neigung zum Verbrechen, zur Gewalt, zum Rauben und Morden, haben. Aber auch die anderen, die eigentlich okay sind, die werden da mitgezogen. Das ist so eines der Phänomene, die sich da beobachten lassen. Und da stellt sich natürlich die Frage, warum das so ist und dann vor allem wie lässt sich das verhindern, in Zukunft, die Wiederholung.

*Sandra Farinelli:* Und da sind Sie dann bei Beuys, bei Joseph Beuys?

*Michael Holst:* Ja. Oder besser gesagt bei der Wirkung, die Beuys auf mich als heranwachsenden Künstler gehabt hat. Also auch wenn ich mich mit dem Werk von Beuys auseinandersetze, es zum Gegenstand meiner Werke mache, bin ich kein Beuys-Spezialist. Ich bin Künstler, kein Kunsthistoriker. Über die Bedeutung von Beuys kann ich nichts sagen, die historische, die kunsthistorische Einschätzung. Ich kann nur sagen wie er, wie sein Werk und die Art wie mit seinem Werk umgegangen wurde und wird auf mich gewirkt hat. In der öffentlichen Diskussion ebbt das ja aktuell stark ab, ist fast ganz verschwunden, ist museal, natürlich in dem Sinne das Museen das bewahren, aber damit verschwindet es auch. Aber als ich anfing Kunst zu machen – also ich war nie ein Schüler von Beuys, nur um dem Missverständnis vorzubeugen, das stand auch mal in einem Artikel über mich, also nein, kein Schüler, ich habe nur in der Zeit gelebt, mich als Künstler entwickelt, als hier in Deutschland Beuys sehr präsent war, dominant, kontrovers, sehr kontrovers, aber auch als epochemachender Künstler. Und das ist natürlich etwas das einen prägt, etwas worauf man reagiert.

*Sandra Farinelli:* Und Ihrer Reaktion sind Bilder von Waschbecken.

*Michael Holst:* Ja ich bin eben Photograph. Und auch wenn ich auch Maler bin und Skulpturen und Installationen machen: In diesem Fall, für dieses Projekt, bin ich Photograph. Und da sind dann ja diese Schüsseln, mit den Rändern des eingetrockneten Wassers, mit diesen Kompositionen aus Seifenlaugenrändern, die Beuys gemacht hat und da sind die Performances und die Rituale. Da war er ja sehr stark drin. Und da geht es um Schuld, um Reinigen, um Reinwaschen und auch darum, dass das nie gelingt. Letzteres ist ein Subtext, den Beuys glaube ich nie gesehen hat, obwohl er in jedem seiner Werken eingeprägt ist, meist sogar sehr deutlich, auch wenn man das in der zeitgenössischen Rezeption meist nicht gesehen hat.

*Sandra Farinelli:* Das ist also, verstehe ich Sie da richtig, eine Neuinterpretation von Beuys? Ein anderer Blick auf ihn.

*Michael Holst:* Nun ja, also das worüber wir hier sprechen, ja vielleicht, soweit man das in so einem Gespräch machen kann, eine Neuinterpretation, das sind ja nur

Gedanken, die ich so habe, bei meiner Arbeit. Aber meine Arbeit und eben auch diese Ausstellung, die sind das natürlich nicht. Erst einmal natürlich weil man da viel zu viel über Beuys wissen müsste, was ich einfach nicht tue, und dann auch natürlich, weil das ja meinen Bildern die Eigenständigkeit nähme. Und das sollte man nie tun, einem Kunstwerk seine Eigenständigkeit nehmen. Die Bilder sind eine Reaktion, sie benutzen einen bestimmten Aspekt der Sprache von Beuys, verwenden sein Vokabular, nehmen auch die Assoziationen auf, die sein Vokabular erzeugt, aber dann machen sie damit etwas neues, etwas von Heute und natürlich gespeist aus dem Blick, aus der Erfahrung der Vergangenheit, dessen was uns ausmacht in unserem Wesen als Gewordene, zum Jetzt hin, und immer nur mit einer Vorstellung, nie mit einer Erfahrung, von Zukunft. Da kommen wir nicht dran.

*Sandra Farinelli:* Also das mit dem Vokabular, mit der Bildsprache, die Sie – ich sage das mal in meinen eigenen Worten – aus der Objekt- aus der Installations-Kunst, herausgenommen haben in die Photographie, das verstehe ich jetzt. Das funktioniert bei mir auch so, beim Betrachten. Das ist auch schon bei mir passiert, als ich das erste Mal Ihre Bilder gesehen habe, so ganz ohne Erklärung. Aber wie gehen Sie da weiter?

*Michael Holst:* Es gibt ja von Beuys diese Erzählung, die er mit seinen Filzprojekten, mit allen Sachen die er mit Filz gemacht hat, immer verknüpft, verbunden hat. Filz ist ja für Ihn ein besonderes Material – und Filz ist, das ist ja Wolle, ineinander geriebene Wolle eigentlich, eben verfilzt, wie man sagen würde – also Filz ist wirklich ein besonderes Material, auch sehr langlebig, wenn man richtig mit ihm umgeht, nichts was man wirklich gut bemalen kann, oder bedrucken, auch wenn das natürlich geht, und das habe ich auch für einige Projekte schon gemacht. Aber Filz hat schon eine sehr eigene Struktur, was ich an Filz liebe. Aber darum geht es jetzt hier nicht. Es geht um die Erzählung. Der abgestürzte Flieger, der von den Kosaken, gefunden wird, in Fett und Filz gepackt und gesundgepflegt. Das sind ja Motive von Menschlichkeit in einer unmenschlichen Situation, in Umständen des Grauens und des Schreckens. Ein Flugzeugabsturz, ein Überlebender. Und das ist das was Beuys immer so erzählt hat. Das aber gar nicht wahr ist. Oder wahr schon, aber eben nicht geschehen. Das hat seine Frau einmal gesagt in einem Interview, und das war eigentlich, oder konnte eigentlich jedem klar sein. Trotzdem war Beuys sehr erfolgreich, mit dieser kleinen Erzählung. Das war einfach eine Geschichte, eine die packte, und das tat sie auch – da wurde drüber gesprochen – weil sie einen Subtext hatte, einen Subtext, der noch eine ganz andere Geschichte transportierte. Der sagte, dass Beuys Soldat war, Flieger, der hat Bomben auf Menschen, auf deren Häuser und Städte, geworfen.

*Sandra Farinelli:* Ist ihm das vorgehalten worden?

*Michael Holst:* Nein. Also soweit ich das weiß nicht. Also wie gesagt, ich bin kein Beuys-Spezialist. Ich kann da nichts Verbindliches oder kunsthistorisch Exaktes zu sagen, so wirklich allgemein. Ich bin da auch nur so Zeitzeuge, mit einem sehr subjektiven Eindruck. Das ist ja das Problem bei oral history, dass jeder so seinen Eindruck erzählt, aber das ist immer sehr subjektiv, und so ist das bei mir auch. Ich kenne nur das, was bei mir angekommen ist. – Also provokativ könnte man sagen: Ich kenne nur die Wirkung, nicht das Werk und natürlich auch nicht den Künstler, so als Mensch. – Doch das muss man gar nicht so provokativ sagen. Okay. – Aber ich habe einiges von Beuys gesehen und in den Ausstellungen ist das natürlich nicht angesprochen worden, das mit dem Krieg und dem Soldat sein und dem Bombenabwerfen. Der war immer Opfer *(holt Luft)*. Es gibt bei Marcel Proust, in der Suche nach der verlorenen Zeit, eine wunderbare Passage, in dem einzigen Teil, in dem er nicht als Ich-Erzähler auftritt, dem Teil in dem Swann im Mittelpunkt steht, der Lebemann Swann, und da sind es Gedanken über die Lüge. Und Odette, die Geliebt Swanns, die lügt, ganz offensichtlich lügt sie, sagt nicht die Wahrheit, das ist ein Teil ihres Geschäftsprinzips, ihres Umgangs mit anderen Menschen, insbesondere mit Männern, und doch ist ihr die Lüge zuwider, sie hält sie nur für eine Notwendigkeit, etwas das man nicht umgehen kann. Und damit die Lüge für sie etwas erträglicher ist, füllt sie sie immer mit Stücken der Wahrheit auf, kleine Dinge die wirklich passiert sind, Sachen die nur eine Randbedeutung haben, aber Swann wird erst dadurch auf die Wahrheit, die verschwiegene oder die mit der Lüge überdeckt Wahrheit hingewiesen. Und so, so sehe ich das, ist das auch bei dieser Filz-Erzählung von Beuys. Er erzählt damit, neben allem was an der Oberfläche erzählt wird, was auf der sichtbaren Ebene steht, eben auch die Geschichte seiner Schuld. Und so verstehe ich dann auch die Waschschüsseln als diesen Versuch, diesen nie glücken könnenden Versuch, der Reinigung. Das sind ja tiefe Traumatisierungen, die da passiert sind.

*Sandra Farinelli:* Sie klingen da ja jetzt fast wie ein Therapeut.

*Michael Holst:* (lacht) Nun, vielleicht muss der Künstler ja manchmal auch ein Therapeut sein. Die Frage ist natürlich ob er das kann, so ganz grundsätzlich, und da würde ich Nein sagen. Aber er kann als Therapeut wirken. Die eigentliche Arbeit macht natürlich der Betrachter, der Zuschauer in einer Ausstellung. Da ist die Kunst nur der Auslöser. Was dann ja gut ist, oder auch okay. – Aber ich bleibe mal noch einen Augenblick bei den Traumatisierungen. Ich finde das wichtig. Also ich hatte mal bei einer meiner Ausstellungen, das war noch eines der frühen Frankfurter Goethe-Projekte, ein sehr intensives und interessantes Gespräch mit einem Psychotherapeuten, schon ein älterer Herr, also viel Berufserfahrung, der war eigentlich schon in Pension, machte aber in der Praxis eines Kollegen noch so einige Stunden in der Woche und der hatte sich auf die Behandlung von Traumpatienten spezialisiert. Und der meinte, dass man, wenn man eine Traumatisierung erfahren hat, das immer wiederholen will, das gar nicht, wie man eigentlich vielleicht vermuten könnte, meiden will, das irgendwie auch, aber ganz tief im Inneren ruft einen das Trauma immer wieder. Und man geht, man stolpert, gerade wenn man es ganz massiv vermeiden will, ganz unversehen immer wieder da hinein. Der Sinn dahinter ist, dass man sich zeigen will, dass man es aushalten kann, dieses Fürchterliche. Also ich denke bei Beuys ist das genau dieser Punkt. Er konnte seine traumatische Situation, auch das Schuldig werden, verletzt und schuldig, immer wieder erzählen, in einer transformierten Weise und deshalb war es für ihn und auch für seine Zuhörer so mächtig.

*Sandra Farinelli:* Aber Sie haben nicht diese Kriegserfahrungen, nicht diese Traumatisierungen. Doch bei Ihnen kommen die Waschbecken auch immer wieder. Zweiundsiebzig Bilder waren es im ersten Band und jetzt sind es, Sie nennen die Zahl im Titel nicht, aber ich habe einfach mal die Ausstellung durchgezählt, und ich komme auf 132.

*Michael Holst:* Nun, das mit der Zahl, oder besser, das die
Zahl nicht im Titel steht, das war eine bewusste Entscheidung. Es gab auch eine Phase des Projektes, in
der wir, also ich und mein Team, gedacht haben, dass
wir das wieder mit 72 Bildern machen: „72 neue Bilder
meines Waschbeckens am Morgen" wäre der Titel dann
gewesen. Vielleicht auch „72 neue Bilder meines Waschbeckens am Nachmittag". Und da haben Sie natürlich
die Wiederholung, nach der Sie gefragt haben. Und das
ist ein ganz bewusst gesetztes Motiv. Noch einmal so ein
Projekt, noch einmal diese Bilder, Bilder von solcher
Art, Bilder mit diesem Thema. Weil es eben immer wieder hoch kommt, weil es nicht, noch nicht, immer noch
nicht geklärt ist, auch nach 80 Jahren noch nicht. Und
ja, ich habe die Kriegserfahrung nicht. Und da bin ich
natürlich auch froh drum, dass ich die nicht habe. Das
sucht man sich ja nicht aus, in welche Generation man
geboren wird. Aber, und das ist ein Aber das nicht wertend gemeint ist: Ich bin aufgewachsen mit dem Echo
dieses Krieges, einem sehr mächtigen Echo, viel auch,
an vielen Stellen, unterdrückt, mit großer Gewalt sogar,
und wie das so ist, wenn etwas unterdrückt wird, dann
wirkt sich das wie eine Verstärkung aus, dann kommt es
an einer anderen Stelle mit doppelter Wucht hervor. Eine
Fontaine. Und dann völlig unverstanden. Und dieses
Echo des Krieges war so wie ein Geruch in einem Haus
in dem es gebrannt hat, und das man völlig renoviert hat,
gewaschen, geputzt , die Tapeten heruntergerissen, alles
neue gemacht. Und dann kommt man wieder in dieses
Haus, kommt in den Flur und da ist er immer noch, dieser Geruch. Vielleicht überdeckt von dem synthetischen

Zitronenduft des Reinigers, mit dem gerade noch die neu gelegten glatten Bodenfliesen gewischt worden sind. Aber er ist da. Und so war das auch mit dem Echo des Kriegs, mit dem Echo der Kriegszeit. Das war da. Selbst wenn man das Echo nicht direkt hörte, es schwang bei allem mit, in dieser Generation. Meine Eltern waren die Kinder der Generation die den Krieg gemacht und die ihn erlitten haben. Das ging ja quer durch Familien, die aktiv den Krieg Unterstützenden, die ihn Betreibenden und die, die ihn erlitten, erduldeten und auch die, die gab es ja auch, die versuchten etwas gegen ihn zu tun.

*Sandra Farinelli:* Und warum machen Sie jetzt Waschbeckenbilder?

*Michael Holst:* Nun, das ist eine gute Frage. Also so ganz grundsätzlich könnte ich die gar nicht beantworten. Oder müsste die mit einem Gemeinplatz beantworten: Weil ich bin, weil ich ein Künstler bin, und weil Photographie eine meiner künstlerischen Ausdrucksformen ist. Und weil ich damit Bilder mache, mit denen ich meinen Blick auf Dinge zeigen will, mit denen ich einen neuen, einen anderen Blick auf Dinge, auf Wirklichkeit ermöglichen will. Und hier dann: Aufmerksamkeit für die Verletzlichkeit des Guten, für die Empfindlichkeit der menschlichen Seele und des menschlichen Körpers, der der Träger dieser Seele ist. Und für die Empfindlichkeit der Welt, dieses Systems von Seiendem das den Menschen, das uns, hervorgebracht hat. Und eigentlich sind wir alle eine Einheit, das ganze Leben auf diesem Planeten, und wir, die Menschen, sind da – weil wir nachdenken können, über uns, weil wir reflektieren können – in einer besonderen Position. Wir haben eine besondere Gabe, eine wunderbare besondere Gabe, die so wunderbare Dinge hervorbringen kann wie diese großartigen Kunstwerke zum Beispiel, die wir in unseren Museen und Gotteshäusern, auch in unseren Wohnhäusern und Galerien aufbewahren, die wir für viel Geld kaufen und verkaufen, was ja auch eine Wertschätzung ist. Es ist mir wert, dass ich drei, vier oder auch mehr Jahresgehälter ausgebe, für eine von einem meiner Mitmenschen bemalte Leinwand, ein Stück Holz, das besonders geformt ist, Riemenschneider zum Beispiel, oder Texte, das ist ja alles Kunst. Und wir können darüber nachdenken. Ich komme noch einmal mit Marcel Proust. Da gibt es wunderbare Szenen über das Hören von Musik, deren Wirkung. Er erfindet eine Sonate, die es so gar nicht gibt. Und beschreibt ihre Wirkung. Da wird Liszt gespielt und auf den Gesichtern der Zuhörerinnen zeigt sich das durch langjährigen Klavierunterricht geschulte und herausgebildete Verständnis für diese virtuose und komplizierte Musik. Wunderbare Kunstwerke. Ja und ich hoffe einfach, dass meine Bilder, dass wenn man sie in der Ausstellung sieht, hier und in den kommenden Tagen, oder wenn man sie dann später in dem Ausstellungskatalog noch einmal betrachtet, und später wird es den Katalog dann ja auch als Buch geben, im Buchhandel, dann, dass da einfach etwas entsteht, ein Impuls, und dass diese Spuren geschehener Waschungen, aber auch das nicht gewaschen sein dieses Waschbeckens, das die Sprünge, an denen sich Dreck festgesetzt hat, was vielleicht auch Ekel auslöst, dass das dazu führt, darüber nachzudenken, wie man da tätig werden kann, wie man etwas verändern kann. Und ganz wichtig: Jeder kann etwas verändern und das wünsche ich mir. Dass dann die Wiederholung nicht mehr geschieht, sondern man, sondern wir, es anders machen und dass wir sehen wie es geht, positiv. Das ist so meine Motivation und mein Wunsch.

*Sandra Farinelli:* Ich denke das ist ein wunderbarer Wunsch, den ich jetzt mitnehme in den Gang durch die Ausstellung und dich denke den wir auch alle hier weiter tragen können. Und ganz in diesem Sinne: Vielen Dank für das inspirierende Gespräch.

*Transkription des Gesprächs von Sandra Farinelli und Michael Holst vom 09.04.2025 im Forum72, Basel. Transkription Andrea Wassmanshausen und Claudia Tom. Redaktion Kathrin Schubert.*

# New Washbasin Pictures

*The German-Italian journalist Sandra Farinelli in conversation with Michael Host on the occasion of the opening of the exhibition*
*"Some new pictures of my washbasin"*

*Sandra Farinelli:* Welcome to Art-Forum 72. Thank you for taking the time for this interview. We are in the main room of your new exhibition and in the background one of these oversized pictures. I think it's the largest print here in the installation, two meters eighty by three meters ninety, if I've seen it correctly on the small information board next to the picture. So my first question is quite simple: Is size an issue for you?

*Michael Holst:* Well, it's about spaces and when you do an exhibition, it's about impact. And the images you hang have to fit in, in terms of their size, to the room and to the people who see them. That's always very important to me, the question of where someone is standing when they look at a picture. What is it like when you enter a room, what is it like when you walk through the room. Even if it's an exhibition where there are 'only' pictures hanging on the wall or in the room, that's an important question. It's actually just like an installation, when you stage an experience with objects in the room. It's the same with the presentation of photography. And of course it's great, especially with photography, that you can simply make prints, or inkprints, that's what they are here, especially the large inkprints, in practically any size and on many different materials. And then I can also offer a visitor this huge picture in a dimension that fits in their home or office. I also do office furnishings or reception halls for companies, and the requirements for the format are simply very different, without any judgment, simply functional. It has to fit. And yes, that's why size is important, but size doesn't just mean huge, it means the right size, the right size for the room, and these are very large rooms, so the prints have to be very large.

*Sandra Farinelli:* And then the washbasin. All images are pictures of a washbasin. My thought was, after a few minutes actually, everything yet was not fully set up, but all the pictures were already hanging, and I went there alone, and still without the comments that are now next to the pictures on the wall or on a stand, and then my question was: What kind of washbasin is that? Nowadays, people always ask whether the pictures are real photographs or generated by AI and you have also just completed a project in which you, together with this Japanese programmer ...

*Michael Holst:* ... yes, with Aiko Ito ...

*Sandra Farinelli:* ... yes exactly, this project with the images generated by computer processes.

*Michael Holst:* You mean "the invisible".

*Sandra Farinelli:* Yes. And there's just really this question: What kind of washbasin is that? Is that a real washbasin, one that you use to shave in the morning, for example? I have the impression that you are very well shaved today. You usually wear a beard.

*Michael Holst:* Thank you *(smiles)*.

*Sandra Farinelli:* So this washbasin really exists. Is it in your home? Or did you find it at a landfill site? Or ...

*Michael Holst:* ... So with the landfill, that surprises me now, and at home, that's something that's important to me, to protect the private sphere. Although I am always very personal in my installations and actions, but not private.

*Sandra Farinelli:* But by placing the possessive pronoun in the title you suggest that. Don't you?

*Michael Holst:* Well, yes, of course. But at the same time, it's my decision not to say any more than the images show, or perhaps more precisely, not to say anything at all about this and such questions and to let the images speak for themselves. And if you engage with these images, and also with the title and the texts here in the exhibition, then it can have a good effect and is perhaps also an answer to your question. And yes, of course it's my washbasin. I am the owner. We always have a lawyer on the team for the big projects. That's important and the lawyers always make a difference between possessor and owner. – that's what I have learned already. – As I said, the owner is me. The possessor is my landlord. I rented the studio. And that's why I can't sell this washbasin, it's that simple.

*Sandra Farinelli:* Could you have sold it? Were there any people interested?

*Michael Holst:* Funnily enough, yes. You could dismantle it, of course. But that's not legally possible, of course. I would have to ask the landlord, the owner *(laughs)*. So it's the washbasin in the studio in Cologne. The studio that Marcellus found for me, and there's a washbasin from the 1970s, in the small separate room, and I saw it and then it was an object, and actually only rarely used, but with a development. And that's actually all I can say about it. It's about time, about traces of time, that's one of the themes in there.

*Sandra Farinelli:* I read that you said that these images are anti-war images. What do you mean by that?

*Michael Holst:* I think that's from an interview, the quote you have in mind, from an interview with one of the two big Frankfurt newspapers. I think you read this quote there. They exaggerated it a bit, or pointedly, you could say. It happens sometimes with journalists who want to get to the heart of the matter. So literally, so directly, one-to-one, that's not my wording. Although in terms of content, if you understand it correctly, it is of course completely accurate.

*Sandra Farinelli:* You'll have to explain that, I think.

*Michael Holst:* Well, I said that these images and this exhibition are a statement against war in a very fundamental way. They are against the making and planning and justifying and preparing for war and also a pointed statement against the way in which all the crimes and horrible terriblenesses that are committed in war are later dealt with, and which are the essence of war.

*Sandra Farinelli:* How do you make the connection? Your images – images of a washbasin – and war?

*Michael Holst:* It's a Beuys theme, of course, this thing with the washbasin. That was already the case in the first project, in the 72 pictures, also in the subtitle. And here it's taken up again, very topically. It's a theme, war, 'again', you could say. Here in Europe, the 'again' is correct. Globally, there have always been wars, large and small, and most of them have been forgotten by the global public. Yes, and the way we talk and think about it today, now, here, is, I think, frightening. And that somehow contrasts quite painfully with the way we have talked about dealing with the war or trying to deal with it here in Europe, especially in Germany of course. I always have this 'never again' in my ear. And I think that was meant very seriously. But suddenly, all of a sudden, it faded away, faded into the empty space of a universe that has been given different coordinates, in which people measure with different units of length, very disruptive. And this attempt to protect a society, a continent, perhaps even the world, from people beating each other up again in masses, injuring each other, throwing explosives and highly accelerated sharp-edged metal objects at each other, this attempt, as serious as it was, is a failure, it must be said, even at the very first exposure. *(takes a breath)* We are preparing for war again, waging it. And the "we" here is meant in a very broad sense: we humans. Yet we were so shocked after all the atrocities and crimes, after two world wars. And war is always a crime and it also leads to the innocent, the victims, getting into situations where they think – I say this without any judgment, I don't know whether this is right or wrong from a moral point of view – that they, practically everyone, thinks they have to do something that they would normally consider ethically forbidden. These are really fundamental questions. And of course the people who, for whatever reason, have a tendency towards crime, violence, robbery and murder, live it out. But the others, who are actually okay, are also drawn into it. That's one of the phenomena that can be observed. And that naturally raises the question of why this is happening and, above all, how we can prevent it from happening again in the future.

*Sandra Farinelli:* And that brings you to Beuys, to Joseph Beuys?

*Michael Holst:* Yes. Or rather to the effect that Beuys had on me as an artist growing up. So even though I deal with

Beuys' work and make it the subject of my works, I'm
not a Beuys specialist. I am an artist, not an art histo-
rian. I can't say anything about the significance of Beuys,
the historical, the art-historical assessment. I can only
say what effect he, his work and the way his work was
and is dealt with had on me. In the public debate, it's
ebbing away, it's almost completely disappeared, it's
museum-like, of course, in the sense that museums pre-
serve it, but it's also disappearing. But when I started
making art – well, I was never a student of Beuys, just
to avoid any misunderstanding, that was once written
in an article about me, so no, not a student, I just lived
in the time, developed as an artist, when in Germany
Beuys was very present here, dominant, controversial,
very controversial, but also as an epoch-making artist.
And of course that is something that shapes you, something you react to.

*Sandra Farinelli:* And your reaction is making some images
of washbasins.

*Michael Holst:* Yes, I am a photographer. And even though
I'm also a painter and make sculptures and installations:
In this case, for this project, I am a photographer. And
then there are these bowls, with the edges of the dried
water, with these compositions of soap suds edges that
Beuys made and there are the performances and the
rituals. He was very much into that. And it's about guilt,
about purging, about washing clean and also about the
fact that it never works. The latter is a subtext that I
don't think Beuys ever saw, although it is imprinted in
every one of his works, usually very clearly, even if it is
normally not seen in contemporary reception.

*Sandra Farinelli:* So, am I understanding you correctly, is
this a reinterpretation of Beuys? A different view of him.

*Michael Holst:* Well, what we're talking about here may be, perhaps, as far as you can make it in a conversation like this, a reinterpretation, these are just thoughts that I have while doing my work. But my work and this exhibition, of course, are not intended to be a reinterpretation. First of all, of course, because you would have to know far too much about Beuys, which I simply don't do, and then, of course, because that would take away the independence of my images. And you should never do that, take away the independence of a work of art. The images are a reaction, they use a certain aspect of Beuys' language, they use his vocabulary, they also take up the associations that his vocabulary creates, but then they use it to make something new, something from today and of course fed by the view, from the experience of the past, of what makes us what we are in our essence as grown beings, towards the now, and always only with an idea, never with an experience, of the future. We can't get to that.

*Sandra Farinelli:* So the thing with the vocabulary, the visual language that you – I'll say it in my own words – have taken out of object art, out of installation art, into photography, I understand that now. It works for me, when I look at it. That already happened to me when I saw your images for the first time, without any explanation. But how do you go on from there?

*Michael Holst:* Beuys had this narrative that he always linked to his felt projects, to everything he did with felt. Felt is a special material for him – and felt is, after all, wool, wool rubbed together, felted, as you might say – so felt really is a special material, also very durable if you handle it properly, nothing that you can really paint or print on, even if that is possible of course, and I have already done that for some projects. But felt has a very unique texture, which is what I love about felt. But that's not the point here. It's about the narrative. The downed airman who is found by the Cossacks, wrapped in fat and felt and nursed back to health. These are motifs of humanity in an inhuman situation, in circumstances of horror and terror. A plane crash, a survivor. And that's what Beuys always told us. But it's not true at all. Or true, but it didn't happen. His wife once said that in an interview, and that was actually, or could actually be, clear to everyone. Nevertheless, Beuys was very successful with this little story. It was simply a story, one that grabbed you, and it did – it was talked about – because it had a subtext, a subtext that conveyed a completely different story. It said that Beuys was a soldier, an airman, who dropped bombs on people, on their houses and cities.

*Sandra Farinelli:* Has he been accused of that?

*Michael Holst:* No. Not as far as I know. As I said, I'm not a Beuys specialist. I can't say anything binding or art-historically precise about it in general. I'm just a con-temporary witness with a very subjective impression. That's the problem with oral history, that everyone gives his own impression, but it's always very subjective, and that's how it is for me too. I only know what I received. – So provocatively you could say: I only know the effect, not the work and of course not the artist as a person. – But you don't have to say that so provocatively. Okay. But I've seen a lot of Beuys and of course that wasn't ad-dressed in the exhibitions, the war and being a soldier and dropping bombs. He was always a victim *(takes a breath)*. There's a wonderful passage in Marcel Proust, in The Search for Lost Time, in the only part where he doesn't appear as a first-person narrator, the part where

Swann is at the center, the bon vivant Swann, and there are thoughts about lying. And Odette, Swann's lover, she lies, obviously she lies, she doesn't tell the truth, it's part of her business principle, her dealings with other people, especially men, and yet she dislikes lying, she just thinks it's a necessity, something you can't avoid. And to make the lie a little more bearable for her, she always fills it up with pieces of the truth, little things that really happened, things that only have a marginal significance, but Swann only by these pieces is made aware of the truth, the truth that has been concealed or covered up with the lie. And that, as I see it, is also the case with this felt narrative by Beuys. In addition to everything that is told on the surface, on the visible level, he is also telling the story of his guilt. And so I also understand the washing bowls as this attempt, this attempt at cleansing that can never succeed. These are deep traumatizations that happened there.

*Sandra Farinelli:* You almost sound like a therapist now.

*Michael Holst:* (laughs) Well, perhaps the artist sometimes has to be a therapist. The question of course is whether he can do that, in principle, and I would say no. But he can act as a therapist. Of course, the actual work is done by the viewer, the spectator in an exhibition. The art is just the trigger. Which is fine, or okay. – But I'll stay with traumatization for a moment. I think that's important. At one of my exhibitions, which was one of the early Goethe projects in Frankfurt, I had a very intensive and interesting conversation with a psychotherapist, an older man with a lot of professional experience, who was actually already retired, but still worked a few hours a week in a colleague's practice and specialized in the treatment of trauma patients. And he said that if you've been traumatized, you always want to repeat it, you don't want to avoid it, as you might think, deep down, the trauma steadily keeps calling you. And you go, you stumble into it, again and again quite unintentionally, especially when you want to avoid it so badly. The idea behind it is that you want to show yourself that you can endure it, this terrible thing. So I think that's exactly the point with Beuys. He was able to recount his traumatic situation, including being guilty, hurt and guilty, again and again, in a transformed way and that's why it was so powerful for him and also for his audience.

*Sandra Farinelli:* But you don't have these experiences of war, these traumas. But in your work, the washbasins come up again and again. There were seventy-two pictures in the first volume and now there are, you don't mention the number in the title, but I just counted through the exhibition and I came up with 132.

*Michael Holst:* Well, the number, or rather the fact that the number is not in the title, that was a conscious decision. There was also a phase of the project in which we, me and my team, thought that we would do it again with 72 images: "72 new images of my washbasin in the morning" would have been the title. Or perhaps "72 new images of my washbasin in the afternoon". And then, of course, you have the repetition you asked for. And that is a very deliberate motif. Another project like this, another bundle of these images, images of this kind, images with this theme. Because it comes up again and again, because it has not, not yet, still not been clarified, not even after 80 years. And yes, I don't have the war experience. And of course I'm glad that I don't have it. You don't choose which generation you're born into. But, and this is a but that is not meant in a judgmental way: I grew up with the echo of this war, a very powerful echo, suppressed a lot, in many places, with great violence even, and as it is, when something is suppressed, it has the effect of amplification, then it comes out in another place with double the force. A fountain. And then completely misunderstood. And this echo of the war was like a smell in a house that had burned out and had been completely renovated, washed, cleaned, the wallpaper torn down, everything made new. And then you come back into the house, walk into the hallway and there it still is, that smell. Perhaps masked by the synthetic lemon scent of the cleaner that has just been used to mop the newly laid smooth floor tiles. But it's there. And so it was with the echo of the war, the echo of wartime. It was there. Even if you didn't hear the echo directly, it resonated with everything in that generation. My parents were the children of the generation that made the war and suffered through it. It went right through families, those who actively supported the war, those who waged it and those who suffered it, endured it, and there were also those who tried to do something about it.

*Sandra Farinelli:* And why are you doing washbasin images now?

*Michael Holst:* Well, that's a good question. I couldn't answer it in a fundamental way. Or I would have to answer it with a platitude: Because I am, because I am an artist, and because photography is one of my forms of artistic expression. And because I use it to make images, images that show my view of things, images with which I want to enable a new, different view of things, of reality. And here then: attention to the vulnerability of the good, to the sensitivity of the human soul and the human body, which is the bearer of this soul. And for the sensitivity of the world, this system of being that has brought forth the human being, us. And actually we are all one unit, the whole of life on this planet, and we, the human beings, are there – because we can think, think about ourselves, because we can reflect – in a special position. We have a special gift, a wonderful special gift that can produce such wonderful things as these great works of art, for example, that we keep in our museums and places of worship, also in our homes and galleries, that we buy and sell for a lot of money, which is also an appreciation. It is worth it to me to spend three, four or even more annual salaries on a canvas painted by one of my fellow human beings, a piece of wood that is specially shaped, Riemenschneider for example, or texts, all that is art. And we can think about it. I'll come back to Marcel Proust. There are wonderful scenes about listening to music, its effect. He invents a sonata that doesn't even exist. And describes its effect. Liszt is played and the faces of the listeners show the understanding for this virtuoso and complicated music that has been trained and developed through many years of piano lessons. Wonderful works of art. Yes, and I simply hope that my images, when you see them in the exhibition, here and in the coming days, or when you look at them again later in the exhibition catalog, and later the catalog will also be available as a book, in bookstores, that something will simply emerge, an impulse, and that these traces of washings that have happened, but also the fact that this washbasin has not been washed, that the cracks on which dirt has settled, which perhaps also triggers disgust, that this leads us to think about how we can take action, how we can change something. And very importantly, everyone can change something and that's what my intention is. That the repetition no longer happens, that we instead do it differently and that we see how it works, positively. That's my motivation and my wish.

*Sandra Farinelli:* I think that's a wonderful wish that I'll take with me on my walk through the exhibition and that I think we can all carry forward here. And on that note, thank you very much for the inspiring conversation.

*Transcription of the conversation between Sandra Farinelli and Michael Holst at Forum72, Basel on 09.04.2025. Transcription by Andrea Wassmanshausen and Claudia Tom. Editor: Kathrin Schubert. Translation: Ugur Tomson.*

# the invisible

*Michael Holst interviewed by Gracia Tonero*

*Talk at the opening panel discussion on the podium in
The David and Richardson Gallery New Douglastown,
Boston, June 24, 2024*

*Gracia Tonero:* You call your latest works digital images.
That makes me think of photography. Is that what you
had in mind? Is that what you want spectators to have
in mind?

*Michael Holst:* Yes and no *(smiles apologetically)*. — I see,
that is not a very satisfying answer. — But yes, I want
people to think of photography and that is what I am, a
photographer. I'm a painter, too, and a sculpture and I'm
doing installations. But yes, here I'm the photographer
and that is what people should have in mind.

*Gracia Tonero:* But in this project you don't call your images
photographies.

*Michael Holst:* Yes. And though they pretend to be photography they are not. They are digital images, digitally created images.

*Gracia Tonero:* And that means …

*Michael Holst:* … that of course that is, always is, a difficult
question to know what that means: digital image. If I use
my cell phone to make an image, perhaps for example
of a tree on a meadow. Than it is, first steep, the camera,
just something like a classical camera, very miniatur-
ized, but something not very different form a classical

camera, that creates the image. A lens system and something the focused light is falling on. That's it. Click. It's not a film, like it used to be, for a long time in a camera, yes, it's a digital sensor, lots of sensors on a tiny piece of silicon, but in principle nothing really different from a film. Somehow amazing, really, yes. The film is chemical, the sensor is electronic. That's the only difference. And so most people think: that's it, that's what the image is, but that's not the case. There's a lot of math there involved. Math processing the sensor data.

*Gracia Tonero:* So apart from the math, not much a difference?

*Michael Holst:* Perhaps. *(Shakes his head with a smile.)* No! A great difference. Not negative, not negative at all. But a great difference. You see, for example: I like photographing faces. Real faces and they have wrinkles, maybe circles under the eyes. But my cell phone doesn't allow that. Faces are smooth for my cell phone. You can't change that, not for my cell phone.

*Gracia Tonero:* But you don't make use of your cell phone for your work as an artist?

*Michael Holst:* Sometime I do … *(pauses for a moment with a bright slightly ironical smile on his face.)*

*Gracia Tonero:* Okay.

*Michael Holst:* Yes, you just have to know what you are doing. And of course normally you don't know what the algorithms in the phone are doing, how they work. But that it not so different with the professional cameras, too. It are very complex systems today, these cameras, and the software you are using to develop the images, that's all very complex too.

*Gracia Tonero:* But you now don't want to start talking about Artificial Intelligence?

44

*Michael Holst:* No, well, but I think we perhaps, may be, have to.

*Gracia Tonero:* Okay.

*Michael Holst:* Well firstly of course because at the moment everybody is talking about that. Just again your cell phone. It is using it *(smiles)*. And then of course because these images, the images of this project, were created in a very special way, were computed in a very special way. So this project is about images and computers and of course about the invisible.

*Gracia Tonero:* The invisible?

*Michael Holst:* Yes, the invisible. And that really is amazing and perhaps more important than talking about computers and artificial intelligence: Showing the invisible. And that may be a contradiction, and it indeed is intended to be a contradiction. The contradiction is that what should become, should be made visible.

*Gracia Tonero:* But images are about something you see, something you can see. You can't see the invisible.

*Michael Holst:* Well perhaps you can. Perhaps you should. For example, there's someone sitting on a bench, let's say at a station. Just like that. He's sitting there looking in front of him, or at his cell phone — we talk a lot about cell phones today *(smiles)*. So what is that, what we see there or what is there? What is the story of this man, for example? Is he sitting there because he's waiting for the train, for a train, or for someone who's coming by train and he wants to pick him up. Or is he sitting there because he has a roof over his head here and he doesn't has a roof at home? It's all possible and these are the stories, the things that are real, really important, too. It's what you can't see, what's invisible, the invisible. But there are also the empty streets, squares, empty places and there is

no one there: Invisible. And that is also a story. A story
of someone who is not there, cannot be there, perhaps
should not be there and that is what these images show.
If you look, look longer, at an image like this, then the
stories and the things appear and that is very astonishing. The world is always — I would like to say — "only"
an interpretation, the interpretation that we made of it.

*Gracia Tonero:* And these images are you interpretation? Or
is it the interpretation of a computer? Where does the
computer, the things you do with the computer, come
into play?

*Michael Holst:* Well, very early indeed. *(Pauses for a moment.)* The images turn to be data, in fact at a very early
stage in the process. Already in the camera. It's an image on the sensor surface. An image you could see if you
would open the camera. Something you of course don't
do. That would destroy the camera. But there inside is an
image, a visible image. For a split of a second, usually a
very small split of a second, there is that image on that
sensor. And then it is read out and it turns to be data, it
is processed and stored, normally on a chip.

*Gracia Tonero:* The data is the image?

*Michael Holst:* Yes, somehow. Or more precise, it is a representation of the image. An invisible representation.
You can't see it, even if you would make use of a great
magnifier. And to make it visible again you need an
interpretation.

*Gracia Tonero:* And that interpretation, that interpretation
that makes the invisible visible, is done by the computer?

*Michael Holst:* Well, yes. I like the expression you used in
your question. It's really on the point: The interpretation, the interpretation we do with the computer, makes
the invisible visible. And the magic thing is that we can

change that interpretation, that we can do it in a lot of very different ways. And it is up to us, up to the photographer, to make the choice. He, we, have the choice. Of course we have to have the knowledge, that's of course the prerequisite. And this project is about making aware of that. That's the core.

*Gracia Tonero:* For this project you worked with Aiko Ito.

*Michael Holst:* Yes. She is great. Really fantastic what she is doing. She is magic with code and computers. I just got to know her — indeed accidentally — a few years ago on one of my exhibitions. She was a visitor of one of my presentations in Frankfurt, the Goethe-Project. And now she did all the software stuff for "the invisible".

*Gracia Tonero:* But she is not invisible.

*Michael Holst:* Not at all. She is very present. She did the introduction and though I of course know that that is not what an ordinary gallery goer will expect, it was about code and computers. But she did it in a way that is was understandable, was accessible, for the people interested in art. It worked. That is so amazing. And I think that is what is important. It is about understanding, this project, and so it of course has to be understandable what we are doing.

*Gracia Tonero:* So let me have a try: If I got it right you developed a statistical model that processed your images and that is the basis for a system that generates new images, simply with some lines of code or natural language and the training data were the thons of digital images you had in your personal archive.

*Michael Holst:* Yes.

*Gracia Tonero:* And the images we see in the project, the exhibition and the book, all were generates by that computer system?

*Michael Holst:* Yes. And that is of course why the images have a totally different quality compared to everything else you see in computer generated images. It is of course not a totally automated process. It is a very special software, a very special set of applications, and the artist has a lot to do. A lot of learning processes and a lot of try and error. I had to make my way with the software and Aiko steadily adopted the software to the way I used it, or — especially in the first phase of the development — tried to use it. And that really opened new worlds. And that is what I want the people to discover who encounter the works of this project.

*Gracia Tonero:* I'm just going to make a cut. I now have the keyword "destruction" on my moderation card. I just have the impression that it doesn't fit at all. You have talked so much here about wonderful worlds, about the emergence of new ideas and images from such an incredible treasure trove of images and thoughts, your images and thoughts, and then, and this is also a room in the exhibition, it says "destruction".

*Michael Holst:* Yes, it's great that you say that, that it triggers that in you. It's only a small room in the exhibition, quite small indeed. We just did it with these wonderful plasterboard walls in the gallery. You don't have as much space there as in a museum or an exhibition hall. This project is really just a small project. It's also very much a digital project. But it was important for me that we had our own space, something separate. Because strictly speaking, this part doesn't really belong to the exhibition, to the installation. It is not a part of the project. It is what happened afterwards. It's about protecting and securing.

*Gracia Tonero:* Protecting and securing with destruction?

*Michael Holst:* No, not with destruction but through destruction. Even if that seems to be a contradiction. Nowadays, when you do something with a system as complicated, or rather complex, as a computer, especially if it's a cluster of mainframes, you naturally look at the result and that's what we did. And then you also look at what happens in and with the machine. And then it's quickly said: Oh, he did that with the computer. Today: Artificial Intelligence. That's not his achievement at all. — Okay. People are very quick to attribute these systems an autonomy, a being of their own, they like to see them as an own person. And then it's not the artist's achievement, they say. And I think it definitely is, because this computer — we've talked about it — is also a work of art, something that is art, not just something that produces it. And then of course it is Aiko who did all the programming. And just as with this international painting course project, where Marcellus organized the whole thing with the servers and the software that we needed to work together over the net, in this case it's also the case that we simply used these machines, with which you can organize stock exchange trading and economies, to make art. The computer is something like a paintbrush or a chisel. Quite simply.

*Gracia Tonero:* Yes, I understand that. But why destruction here?

*Michael Holst:* This is somehow — you could call it — a Stanley Kubrick motif. He also destroyed all the sets of his movie 2001, simply so that a movie couldn't be shot there again. And it's the same with this system. I don't want, or I should say, we don't want anyone to be able to do it again. It should be something unique, not repeatable. The value of the pictures should be appreciated.

They are something unique. And so it is this paradox
that destruction has its reason in preservation and appreciation. Yes, that is a paradox or that is art and I think
the same is also in people and I think it would be wonderful if we could use destruction — we also in us have
the urge to do so — in such a way that it leads to preservation, conservation and appreciation. That would be
my wish.

*Gracia Tonero:* Perhaps one more question about the title:
"the invisible". What does that mean? We see images in
the exhibition, in that book, and you can see everything
very clearly. Nothing is out of focus or blurred or covered, or made invisible ...

*Michael Holst: (smiles)* ... well, there is something that is
covered or overlaid. There is this red square that runs
through the arrangement of the images as a motif and
sometimes even over the images. Already at the very beginning, for example, with the man with the backpack.

*Gracia Tonero:* Yes, I saw that, but somehow I didn't perceive it as covering or masking. I think this red square is
just there very naturally.

*Michael Holst:* That's great that it happened that way. And
I think that's exactly one of the things that are important for me. The making something invisible, the hiding
and the concealing, that is — and not at all negative, in
general — one of the great abilities of human beings.
It is also the ability — conversely speaking — to focus
on what is important. If we didn't block out so much of
what we encounter in our lives, we wouldn't be able to
live at all. It makes sense that our visual perception is
concentrated on the area in front of us. Simply because
of the biological construction of our eyes. We don't have
an angle of vision of 360 degrees, an all-round view, and

we wouldn't be able to process that. Hearing is different. We can also hear what is happening behind us and that is of course important, vital for survival, but our vision is already focused and therefore limited. Our construction of the world works by omission. At the same time, there is the danger that we then, with this actually sensible and good mechanism, also omit something that is important for us.

*Gracia Tonero:* And hence the title?

*Michael Holst:* Yes. So it's quite simple, of course. "the invisible" has several meanings. If you try to translate it into German — German is my mother tongue and then of course if you're working in a language you've learned, I don't want to say a foreign language, I find the word "foreign" inappropriate — so if you do it in a certain language — and I like to work in English a lot, then you're much more sensitive to such diverse possible interpretations of meaning. So in German you would have to decide whether it means "the invisible", in the sense that it means people who are invisible, or whether it means "the invisible", i.e. things that are not visible.

*Gracia Tonero:* And is it now about "things" or about "people"?

*Michael Holst:* Of course it's both *(smiles)*. That's very clear to me. That's why I love this title so much. And of course there are things to be seen in the pictures, the things around us. But maybe you don't see what these things are, what they really are, in the pictures. It is only the visual impression and then from a very specific perspective, a very specific image of the world, of reality. Such an image cannot be anything other than what we have in our heads as an image — meant here in a figurative sense — as a model of the world of the environment.

And thus we confirm our view of the world again and again. And that's why photography is so dangerous as an art form. Because it, i.e. photography, confirms to us again and again that what we see is the way we see it. And with these many images that we now create, mostly just for fun or because that's how it works, with the new computer programs, with Artificial Intelligence, we are also constantly confirming our world. As fantastic or surreal or whatever the images may be, they are always world-confirming images, they fill in a defined image of the image, in this case and that is calculated on the basis of patterns that have been filtered out of an admittedly huge data set. Something new, something different, a new view of the world cannot exist in this system, we are blocking it. But that is precisely the task of art, to make visible what is not visible. Because it may be that our image of the world is wrong, incomplete or in some parts even blatantly wrong and that we are therefore doing the wrong things, that we are therefore driving our cars and polluting the environment, destroying our livelihoods. We want to have fun, a good life and we are destroying it. 50 degrees Celsius in the shade is really too hot for our bodies. We evaporate more liquid than we can drink. You can't survive that. But we ignore it. We buy air conditioning and then we make the greenhouse effect even greater. Because we consume even more energy. It's only a little cooler locally in our small living room, for a time, just a short time. And that's why we have to see the world differently, so that we act differently. There are solutions but we don't apply them and that's because we're looking at the world the wrong way. I know I sound like a climate educator now. But maybe we all need to become climate educators.

*Gracia Tonero:* Is it now more the people — that would be the climate educator — who are at the center of the current project or the things, the invisible, the unseen things that are at the center?

*Michael Holst:* Both. We are also things in the world. — So that's a dangerous sentence, you can't say it like that, you shouldn't say it like that. That's how it's done in business, human capital, it's very dangerous, it's inhumane. But of course, and this is probably the right way to say it, we are also, as one of several traits, material in nature. We are matter, physicality. And as an artist, I work with physicality, with matter. When I apply paint to the canvas, quite classically visible to everyone, when I make a sculpture out of stone or wood or plaster, clay and so on. I give matter a form. And so we humans are also shaped. — That's why art is so important to us, because we find ourselves in it, rediscover ourselves, perhaps even reinvent ourselves — and even when I take photographs, it's something material, the photons of light that I direct onto the film with a lens system, or onto the sensor of my camera in the case of digital photography, that is also matter, and all the processes — and that's why I find digital photography so fascinating — with which I then process this impression of light, still very materially, on machines that consume a lot of energy, but then it takes place with something as abstract as mathematics. And that is something just too magical. This purely mental activity of mathematical thinking, of calculating, of computing, this abstract idea of numbers and counting, that creates images. And hence my thought that the invisible becomes visible in the result of a visible image. I look at one of these images that have been created digitally. They are the result of a huge, unimaginably long computational process — it would be an idea to print out all the operations that are carried out for a single one of these images, simply as a string of characters on paper, just as a typewriter would write it down, that would be tons of pages, a whole library. — And so each of these images is the library of a world. And that's what they show and they refer to what they don't show, to what is invisible, just in the original meaning of the word: invisible. And so I hope that they change our view, our thinking and — this is very important — our actions.

# un-sichtbar

*Deutsche Übersetzung des Gesprächs bei der Eröffnungsdiskussion der Ausstellung „the invisible" auf dem Podium in „The David and Richardson Galery" New Douglastown, Boston, 24. Juni 2024*

*Gracia Tonero:* Sie nennen Ihre neuesten Arbeiten digitale Bilder. Das lässt mich an Photographie denken. Ist das das, was Sie im Sinn hatten? Ist es das, was Besucher assoziieren sollen?

*Michael Holst:* Ja und nein *(lächelt entschuldigend).* – Ich sehe schon, das ist keine sehr befriedigende Antwort. – Aber ja, ich möchte, dass die Leute an Photographie denken, und das ist es, was ich bin, ein Photograph. Ich bin auch ein Maler und ein Bildhauer und mache Installationen. Aber ja, hier bin ich der Photograph, und das ist es, was die Leute im Kopf haben sollten.

*Gracia Tonero:* Aber in diesem Projekt hier, nennen Sie Ihre Bilder nicht Photographien.

*Michael Holst:* Ja. Und obwohl sie vorgeben, Photographie zu sein, sind sie es nicht. Es sind digitale Bilder, digital erzeugte Bilder.

*Gracia Tonero:* Und das bedeutet ...

*Michael Holst:* ... dass es natürlich immer eine schwierige Frage ist, zu wissen, was das bedeutet: digitales Bild. Wenn ich mein Handy benutze, um ein Bild zu machen, vielleicht zum Beispiel von einem Baum auf einer Wiese. Dann ist es, erster Schritt, die Kamera, so etwas wie ein klassischer Photoapparat, sehr miniaturisiert, ja, aber etwas, das sich nicht sehr von einer klassischen Kamera unterscheidet, die das Bild macht. Ein Linsensystem und etwas, auf das das fokussierte Licht fällt. Das war's. Klick. Es ist kein Film, wie es lange Zeit bei der Kamera war, ja, es ist ein digitaler Sensor, ganz viele Sensoren auf einem kleinen Stückchen Silizium, aber im Prinzip nichts anderes als ein Film. Der Film ist chemisch, der Sensor elektronisch. Und damit denken die meisten Leute, dass es das war, dass dann da das Bild ist, aber das ist nicht so. Da kommt dann nämlich noch ganz viel Mathematik dazu. Mathematik, die die Sensordaten verarbeitet.

*Gracia Tonero:* Also, bis auf die Mathematik, kein großer Unterschied?

*Michael Holst:* Vielleicht. *(Schüttelt den Kopf mit einem Lächeln.)* Nein! Ein großer Unterschied. Nicht negativ, ganz und gar nicht negativ. Aber ein großer Unterschied. Sehen Sie zum Beispiel: Ich photografiere gerne Gesichter. Echte Gesichter, Gesichter die Falten haben, vielleicht Ringe unter den Augen. Aber mein Handy lässt das nicht zu. Gesichter sind für mein Handy glatt. Das kann man nicht ändern, nicht für mein Handy.

*Gracia Tonero:* Aber Sie benutzen nicht das Mobiltelefon für Ihre Arbeit als Künstler?

*Michael Holst:* Manchmal mache ich das … *(macht eine kleine Pause mit einem leicht ironischen Lächeln auf dem Gesicht).*

*Gracia Tonero:* Okay.

*Michael Holst:* Ja, man muss nur wissen was man macht. Und natürlich weiß man normalerweise nicht was die Algorithmen auf dem Telefon machen, wie sie funktionieren. Aber das ist auch nicht so viel anders bei den professionellen Kamerasystemen. Das sind sehr komplexe Systeme heute. Und die Software, die man benutzt, um die Bilder zu entwickeln, das ist auch alles sehr komplex.

*Gracia Tonero:* Aber Sie wollen jetzt nicht anfangen über künstliche Intelligenz zu sprechen?

*Michael Holst:* Nein, aber ich denke, vielleicht, müssen wir das tun.

*Gracia Tonero:* Okay.

*Michael Holst:* Na ja, zunächst einmal weil im Moment jeder darüber spricht. Einfach wieder das Handy. Das nutzt das *(lächelt)*. Und dann natürlich weil diese Bilder, die Bilder dieses Projekts, auf eine ganz bestimmte Art erzeugt worden sind, sie wurden auf eine ganz besondere Art berechnet. Es ist so, dass es bei diesem Projekt um Bilder und Computer geht und natürlich um das Unsichtbare.

*Gracia Tonero:* Das Unsichtbare?

*Michael Holst:* Ja, das Unsichtbare. Und das ist wirklich erstaunlich und vielleicht wichtiger als über Computer und künstliche Intelligenz zu sprechen: Das Unsichtbare zu zeigen. Und das kann vielleicht ein Gegensatz sein, und in der Tat ist es beabsichtigt, dass das ein Gegensatz ist. Der Gegensatz ist das was sichtbar werden soll, was sichtbar gemacht werden soll.

*Gracia Tonero:* Aber bei Bildern geht es um etwas das man sieht, das man sehen kann. Das Unsichtbare kann man nicht sehen.

*Michael Holst:* Vielleicht können Sie es. Vielleicht sollten sie es. Zum Beispiel sitzt da jemand auf einer Bank, sagen wir in einem Bahnhof. Einfach so. Er sitzt da und schaut vor sich hin, oder auf sein Handy. – Wir sprechen heute viel über Handys *(lächelt)*. Also was ist das, das was wir da sehen oder das was da ist? Was ist die Geschichte von diesem Mann, zum Beispiel. Sitzt er da, weil er auf den

Zug, auf einen Zug, wartet, oder auf jemanden der mit dem Zug kommt und den er abholen will. Oder sitzt er da, weil er hier ein Dach über dem Kopf hat, ein Dach das er zuhause nicht hat. Das ist ja alles möglich und das sind die Geschichten, die Dinge, die wirklich sind, wirklich wichtig auch. Das ist das was man nicht sieht, das was unsichtbar ist, das Unsichtbare. Aber es sind auch die leeren Straßen, Plätze, leeren Orte und da ist niemand: Unsichtbar. Und das ist auch eine Geschichte. Eine Geschichte von jemandem der nicht da ist, nicht da sein kann, vielleicht auch nicht da sein soll und das zeigen diese Bilder auch. Wenn man schaut, länger schaut, auf so ein Bild, denn kommen da die Geschichten und die Dinge und das ist dann sehr erstaunlich. Die Welt ist immer – ich möchte sagen – „nur" eine Interpretation, die Interpretation die wir uns von ihr machen.

*Gracia Tonero:* Und diese Bilder sind Ihre Interpretation? Oder ist es die Interpretation eines Computers? Wo kommt da der Computer, das was Sie mit dem Computer machen, ins Spiel?

*Michael Holst:* Nun, in der Tat sehr früh. *(Hält einen Moment inne.)* Die Bilder werden zu Daten, und zwar in einem sehr frühen Stadium des Prozesses. Sie sind bereits in der Kamera. Es ist ein Bild auf der Sensoroberfläche. Ein Bild, das Sie sehen könnten, wenn Sie die Kamera öffnen würden. Was Sie natürlich nicht tun. Das würde die Kamera zerstören. Aber im Inneren ist ein Bild, ein sichtbares Bild. Für den Bruchteil einer Sekunde, normalerweise für einen sehr kleinen Bruchteil einer Sekunde, ist dieses Bild auf dem Sensor. Und dann wird es ausgelesen und zu Daten, es wird verarbeitet und gespeichert, normalerweise auf einem Chip.

*Gracia Tonero:* Die Daten sind das Bild?

*Michael Holst:* Ja, irgendwie schon. Oder genauer gesagt, es ist eine Repräsentation des Bildes. Eine unsichtbare Repräsentation. Man kann es nicht sehen, selbst wenn man eine große Lupe benutzen würde. Und um es wieder sichtbar zu machen, braucht man eine Interpretation.

*Gracia Tonero:* Und diese Interpretation, diese Interpretation die das Unsichtbare sichtbar macht, wird vom Computer vorgenommen?

*Michael Holst:* Nun, ja. Mir gefällt der Begriff, den Sie in Ihrer Frage verwendet haben. Er trifft es wirklich auf den Punkt: Die Interpretation, die Interpretation, die wir mit dem Computer machen, macht das Unsichtbare sichtbar. Und das Magische daran ist, dass wir diese Interpretation verändern können, dass wir das auf viele verschiedene Arten tun können. Und es liegt an uns, an dem Photografen, die Wahl zu treffen. Er, wir, haben die Wahl. Natürlich müssen wir das Wissen haben, das ist natürlich die Voraussetzung. Und bei diesem Projekt geht es darum, sich das bewusst zu machen. Das ist der Kern.

*Gracia Tonero:* Für dieses Projekt haben Sie mit Aiko Ito zusammengearbeitet.

*Michael Holst:* Ja. Sie ist großartig. Wirklich fantastisch, was sie da macht. Sie ist magisch mit Code und Computern. Ich habe sie – tatsächlich zufällig – vor ein paar Jahren auf einer meiner Ausstellungen kennengelernt. Sie war eine Besucherin einer meiner Präsentationen in Frankfurt, das Goethe-Projekt. Und jetzt hat sie die ganze Software für „the invisible" gemacht.

*Gracia Tonero:* Aber sie ist nicht unsichtbar.

*Michael Holst:* Ganz und gar nicht. Sie ist sehr präsent. Sie hat die Einführung gemacht, und obwohl ich natürlich weiß, dass das nicht das ist, was ein normaler

Galeriebesucher erwartet, ging es um Code und Computer. Aber sie hat es so gemacht, dass es für die Kunstinteressierten verständlich und zugänglich war. Es hat funktioniert. Das ist wirklich erstaunlich. Und ich denke, das ist es, was wichtig ist. Bei diesem Projekt geht es um das Verstehen, und deshalb muss es natürlich verständlich sein, was wir tun.

*Gracia Tonero:* Lassen Sie es mich mal versuchen: Wenn ich es richtig verstanden habe, haben Sie ein statistisches Modell entwickelt, das Ihre Bilder verarbeitet und das die Grundlage für ein System ist, das Bilder erzeugt, einfach mit einigen Zeilen Code oder natürlicher Sprache und die Trainingsdaten waren die tausende von digitalen Bildern, die Sie in Ihrem persönlichen Archiv hatten

*Michael Holst:* Ja.

*Gracia Tonero:* Und die Bilder, die wir in dem Projekt, der Ausstellung und dem Buch, sehen, wurden alle von diesem Computersystem erzeugt?

*Michael Holst:* Ja. Und das ist natürlich der Grund, warum die Bilder eine ganz andere Qualität haben als alles Andere, was man heute bei computergenerierten Bildern sieht. Es handelt sich natürlich nicht um einen völlig automatisierten Prozess. Es ist eine sehr spezielle Software, ein sehr spezieller Satz von Anwendungen, und der Künstler hat eine Menge zu tun. Viele Lernprozesse und viel Versuch und Irrtum. Ich habe mir meinen Weg mit der Software erst suchen müssen und Aiko hat die Software immer wieder angepasst an die Art wie ich sie benutzt habe, oder besser gesagt – besonders in der ersten Phase der Entwicklung – versucht habe sie zu benutzen. Und das hat wirklich neue Welten eröffnet. Und das ist es, was ich möchte, dass die Menschen entdecken, wenn sie den Werken dieses Projekts begegnen.

*Gracia Tonero:* Ich mache mal einen Cut. Ich habe hier jetzt das Stichwort „Zerstörung" auf meiner Moderationskarte stehen. Ich habe gerade den Eindruck, dass das gar nicht passt. Sie haben jetzt hier so viel von wunderbaren Welten von der Entstehung neuer Ideen und Bilder aus einem so unfassbar großen Schatz von Bildern und Gedanken, Ihren Bildern und Gedanken, erzählt und dann, und das ist ja auch in der Ausstellung ein Raum, da steht „Zerstörung".

*Michael Holst:* Ja, das ist schön, dass Sie das so sagen, dass das das so bei Ihnen auslöst. Das ist in der Ausstellung nur ein kleiner Raum. Wir haben das einfach mit diesen wunderbaren Rigipswänden gemacht, in der Galerie. Da hat man ja nicht so viel Platz, wie in einem Museum oder in einer Ausstellungshalle. Dieses Projekt ist ja wirklich nur ein kleines Projekt. Es ist ja viel auch ein digitales Projekt. Aber es war mir wichtig, dass wir da einen eigenen Raum haben, etwas Abgetrenntes. Denn genau genommen gehört dieser Teil nicht mehr zu der Ausstellung, zu der Installation. Er ist nicht mehr Teil des Projektes. Es ist das, was danach passiert ist. Es geht um das Beschützen, um das Sichern.

*Gracia Tonero:* Beschützen und Sicher mit Zerstörung?

*Michael Holst:* Nein, nicht mit Zerstörung sondern durch Zerstörung. Auch wenn das ein Widerspruch zu sein scheint. Es ist ja heute so, dass wenn man etwas mit einem so komplizierte oder vielleicht besser gesagt komplexen System macht wie mit einem Computer, zumal wenn es sich um ein Cluster von Großrechnern handelt, dann schaut man einmal natürlich auf das Ergebnis und das haben wir ja gemacht. Und dann schaut man aber auch auf das was da in und mit der Maschine passiert. Und dann heißt es schnell: Ach das hat er mit dem

Computer gemacht. Heute: Künstliche Intelligenz. Das ist ja gar nicht seine Leistung. – Okay. – Man spricht diesen Systemen gerne ja sehr schnell eine Eigenständigkeit, ein eigenes Wesen zu, sieht sie gerne auch als eigene Person. Und dann ist es nicht die Leistung des Künstlers, sagt man. Und ich denke: Ist es doch! Denn dieser Computer – wir haben ja drüber gesprochen – ist ja auch ein Kunstwerk, etwas das Kunst ist, nicht nur etwas das sie hervorbringt. Und dann ist das natürlich Aiko, die diese ganze Programmierung gemacht hat. Und so wie bei diesem internationalen Malkursprojekt, wo Marcellus die ganze Sache mit den Servern organisiert hat und der Software, die wir gebraucht haben für die Zusammenarbeit über das Netz, so ist das in diesem Fall auch, dass da einfach wir mit diesen Maschinen, mit denen man Börsenhandel und Wirtschaften organisieren kann, dass wir damit eben Kunst gemacht haben. Der Computer ist da ein Pinsel oder ein Meißel. Ganz einfach.

*Gracia Tonero:* Ja, das verstehe ich. Aber warum dann Zerstörung?

*Michael Holst:* Das ist so – man könnte sagen – ein Stanley Kubrick Motiv. Der hat ja auch alle Kulisse seines Films 2001 zerstört, einfach damit darin nicht noch einmal ein Film gedreht werden kann. Und so ist das auch mit diesem System. Ich will nicht, oder ich müsste sagen, wir wollen nicht, dass das noch jemand noch mal machen kann. Es soll etwas einmalige sein, nicht wiederholbar. Der Wert der Bilder soll dadurch gewertschätzt werden. Sie sind etwas Einmaliges. Und so ist es dann dieses Paradox, dass Zerstörung ihren Grund in Erhalten und Wertschätzung hat. Ja das ist Paradox oder das ist Kunst und dasselbe denke ich ist auch im Menschen und ich denke es wäre etwas wunderbares, wenn wir Zerstörung

– dazu haben wir ja auch den Drang in uns – so einsetzen könnten, dass sie zum Bewahren zum Erhalten zum Wertschätzen führt. Das wäre so mein Wunsch.

*Gracia Tonero:* Vielleicht dann noch eine Frage zum Titel: „the invisible". Was ist damit gemeint? Wir sehen diese Bilder da, in der Ausstellung, in dem Buch, und da sieht man alles sehr genau. Da ist nichts unscharf oder verschwommen oder abgedeckt, oder unsichtbar gemacht …

*Michael Holst: (lächelt)* … nun ja, also abgedeckt oder überdeckt ist da schon etwas. Da ist das rote Quadrat, das als Motiv durch das Arrangement der Bilder geht und manchmal eben auch über die Bilder. Ganz am Anfang zum Beispiel schon bei dem Mann mit dem Rucksack.

*Gracia Tonero:* Ja, das habe ich gesehen, aber irgendwie nicht als ein Überdecken oder Abdecken wahrgenommen. Ich finde dieses rote Quadrat ist einfach sehr natürlich da.

*Michael Holst:* Das ist ja schön, dass das so passiert ist. Und ich denke das ist genau einer der Sachen die mir wichtig ist. Das Unsichtbar-machen, das Verstecken und das Verdecken das ist – und gar nicht negativ, so allgemein – eine der großen Fähigkeiten des Menschen. Das ist ja auch die Fähigkeit – umgekehrt gesprochen – sich auf das was wichtig ist zu fokussieren. Wenn wir nicht ganz viel ausblenden würden in unserem Leben, von dem was uns begegnet, dann könnten wir gar nicht leben. Es hat schon einen Sinn, dass unsere visuelle Wahrnehmung auf den Bereich vor uns konzentriert ist. Einfach schon von der biologischen Konstruktion unserer Augen. Wir haben ja nicht einen Blickwinkel von 360 Grad, so einen Rundumblick. Das könnten wir auch gar nicht verarbeiten. Beim Hören ist das anders. Da können wir auch hören was hinter uns passiert und das ist natürlich wichtig, überlebenswichtig, aber das Sehen ist schon fokussiert, damit auch eingeschränkt. Unsere Konstruktion von Welt funktioniert durch Weglassen. Gleichzeitig ist da die Gefahr, dass wir dann, mit diesem eigentlich sinnvollen und guten Mechanismus, auch etwas weglassen was wichtig ist für uns.

*Gracia Tonero:* Und deshalb der Titel?

*Michael Holst:* Ja. Also ganze einfach natürlich. „the invisible" das hat ja mehrere Bedeutungen. Wenn man versucht das ins Deutsche zu übersetzten – Deutsch ist ja meine Muttersprache und da ist man dann natürlich wenn man in einer gelernten Sprache, ich will nicht sagen in einer Fremdsprache, das Wort „fremd" finde ich unpassend – also wenn man das in einer bestimmten Sprache macht – und ich arbeite ja gerne und viel auf Englisch, dann ist man da viel sensibler für solche vielfältigen Bedeutungsinterpretationsmöglichkeiten. Also im Deutschen müsste man sich entscheiden ob des „die Unsichtbaren" hieße, so in dem Sinne, dass es Personen, Menschen, sind die unsichtbar sind, oder ob es „das Unsichtbare" heißt, also Dinge die nicht sichtbar sind.

*Gracia Tonero:* Und geht es jetzt um „Dinge" oder um „Menschen"?

*Michael Holst:* Es ist natürlich beides *(lächelt)*. Das ist für mich ganz klar. Deshalb liebe ich diesen Titel so. Und es sind natürlich Dinge auf den Bildern zu sehen, die Dinge um uns. Aber vielleicht sieht man das, was diese Dinge sind, das was sie eigentlich was sie wirklich sind, nicht auf den Bilder. Es ist nur der visuelle Eindruck und dann aus einer ganz bestimmten Perspektive, ein ganz bestimmte Bild von Welt, von Wirklichkeit. So ein Bild kann gar nicht anders sein als das was wir als

Bild – hier im übertragenen Sinne gemeint – als Modell von Welt, von Umwelt im Kopf haben. Und damit bestätigen wir uns immer wieder unsere Sicht auf Welt. Und deshalb ist das Photografieren auch so gefährlich, als Kunstform. Weil sie, also die Photografie, uns immer wieder bestätigt, dass das was wir sehen so ist wie wir es sehen. Und mit diesen vielen Bildern, die wir jetzt, meist einfach zum Vergnügen oder weil es eben geht, jetzt mit den neuen Computerprogrammen, erzeugen mit Künstlicher Intelligenz, da bestätigen wir uns auch immer wieder unsere Welt. So phantastisch oder surreal oder was auch immer die Bilder sein mögen, sie sind immer Weltbestätigungsbilder, sie einspringen einem definierten Bild von dem Bild, in diesem Fall und das wird berechnet aufgrund von Mustern, die aus einem, zugegebenermaßen riesigen, Datensatz herausgefiltert worden sind. Etwas neues, etwas andres, einen neuen Blick auf Welt, den kann es da nicht geben, den verbauen wir uns. Aber das gerade ist die Aufgabe von Kunst, das was nicht sichtbar ist sichtbar zu machen. Denn es kann ja sein, dass unser Bild von Welt falsch ist, unvollständig oder in einigen Teile sogar richtig krass falsch und das wir deshalb das Falsche tunt, das wir deshalb mit dem Auto fahren und die Umwelt verschmutzen, unsere Lebensgrundlage zerstören. Wir wollen Spaß haben, ein gutes Leben und wir zerstören das. 50 Grad Celsius im Schatten, das ist wirklich zu heiß für unseren Körper. Wir verdunsten da mehr Flüssigkeit als wir uns durch Trinken zuführen können. Das kann man nicht überleben. Aber wir blenden das aus. Wir kaufen eine Klimaanlage und damit machen wir den Treibhauseffekt noch größer. Weil wir noch mehr Energie verbrauchen. Nur lokal in unserem kleinen Wohnzimmer ist es dann etwas kühler, für eine Zeit, eine kurze Zeit nur. Und deshalb müssen wir die Welt anders sehen, damit wir anders handeln. Es gibt dies Lösungen aber wir wenden sie nicht an und das ist weil wir falsch auf die Welt schauen. Ich weiß ich klinge jetzt wie ein Klimapädagoge. Aber vielleicht müssen wir alle Klimapädagogen werden.

*Gracia Tonero:* Sind es denn jetzt mehr die Menschen – das wäre ja der Klimapädagoge – die bei dem aktuellen Projekt im Mittelpunkt stehen oder die Dinge, die unsichtbaren, die nicht gesehenen Dinge, die Im Mittelpunkt stehen?

*Michael Holst:* Beides. Wir sind ja auch Dinge in der Welt. – Also das ist ein gefährlicher Satz, den kann man so nicht sagen, den sollte man so nicht sagen. In der Wirtschaft macht man das so, human capital, das ist sehr gefährlich, ist menschenverachtend. Aber natürlich und das ist wohl die richtigere Art das zu sagen, sind wir auch, als einer von mehreren Wesenszügen, dinglicher Natur. Wir sind Materie, Körperlichkeit. Und als Künstler arbeite ich mit der Körperlichkeit, mit der Materie. Wenn ich Farbe auf die Leinwand auftrage, ganz klassisch sichtbar für jeden, wenn ich eine Skulptur mache, aus Stein oder Holz oder Gips, Ton und so. Ich gebe der Materie eine Form. Und so sind wir Menschen auch Geformte. – Deshalb ist die Kunst ja für uns so wichtig, weil wir uns in ihr finden, wiederfinden, vielleicht auch wiedererfinden. – Und auch wenn ich photografiere, ist das ja etwas Materielles, die Photonen des Lichtes, das ich mit einem Linsensystem auf den Film, bei der digitalen Photografie, auf den Sensor meiner Kamera lenke, das ist ja auch Materie, und alle die Prozesse – und da finde ich die digitale Photographie so faszinierend – mit denen ich dann, immer noch sehr materiell, diesen Lichteindruck verarbeite, auf Maschinen die viel Energie verbrauchen, da findet das dann aber mit so etwas abstraktem wie Mathematik statt. Und das ist etwas gerade zu zauberhaftes. Dieses rein geistige Tätigsein des mathematischen Denkens, des Kalkulierens, des Berechnens, diese abstrakte Vorstellung von Zahl und Zählen, das macht Bilder. Und deshalb auch mein Gedanke, dass da in dem Ergebnis eines sichtbaren Bildes Unsichtbares sichtbar wird. Es wird sichtbar gemacht beim Sehen. Ich schaue auf eines diese Bilder die digital erzeugt worden sind. Die das Ergebnis eines riesigen eines unvorstellbar langen Rechenprozesse sind – man müsst einmal alle Operationen die ausgeführt werden für ein einziges dieser Bilder ausdrucken, einfach als Zeichenfolge auf Papier so wie eine Schreibmaschine das aufschreiben würde, das wären Unmengen von Seiten, eine ganze Bibliothek. – Und so ist jedes dieser Bilder die Bibliothek einer Welt. Und das zeigen sie und sie verweisen damit auf das was sie nicht zeigen auf das was unsichtbar ist, ganz im ursprünglichen Sinne des Wortes: un-sichtbar. Und damit hoffe ich, dass sie verändern, unseren Blick unser Denke und – das ist ganz wichtig – unser Handeln.

# 142.129 Wäscheständer in der Wüste

*Statements und Aussagen von Michael Holst zu seinem Projekt 142.129 Wäscheständer in der Wüste von Nevada. Projekt einer Installation für Christo und Jeanne-Claude.*

## _ meditativ

„Ich will da keinem zu nahe treten, und viele Leute werden das jetzt vielleicht auch falsch verstehen, aber ich finde Haushalt und Hausarbeit können durchaus meditativ sein. Ich mache das manchmal sogar ganz gerne. Also es kommt natürlich darauf an, wie man das macht, machen kann. Und es muss auch nicht zu häufig sein. *(lacht)* Wenn man Stress hat, dann ist das natürlich stressig. Aber egal.“

*[Michael Holst im Gespräch mit Markus Laatz auf der Konferenz „Zukunft X2“ am 24.11.2018 in Bonn.]*

## _ echo

„Ich habe einmal darüber nachgedacht, ganz klassisch, an einem Samstag, beim Aufhängen der Wäsche der Woche, wie viele Wäscheständer ich so schon vollgehängt habe, in meinem Leben. Also als Kind habe ich das auch schon ab und zu gemacht, die Wäsche aufhängen. Ich fand das ganz witzig. Meine Mutter und mein Vater gingen mit einer großen Wanne in den Keller. Da waren in einem Raum, der Trockenraum hieß, an Haken in der Wand quer durch den Raum, Leinen gespannt. Als Kind waren die natürlich unendlich hoch für mich. Mein Vater und meine Mutter haben die großen Wäschestücke, zum Beispiel die Bettlaken, vorher ausgeschüttelt und stramm gezogen, damit sie schon auf der Leine glatt trockneten. Das war eine richtige Technik. Einer nahm das Laken oben, der andere unten, es wurde mit beiden Händen, die waren eng beieinander, zwischen den beiden Personen stramm gezogen und dann zogen bei beiden Personen gleichzeitig die Hände ganz schnell auseinander. Wenn man das gut machte, dann gab es einen richtigen Knall. Ich fand das faszinierend. Das war eine beeindruckende Aktion, für mich als Kind. Später wurde die getrocknete Wäsche dann abgenommen und noch einmal geschüttelt und stramm gezogen. Dabei entstand viel Bewegung in der Luft, wenn die großen Laken geschüttelt und hin und her gezogen wurden. Als ich etwas größer war und genug Kraft in den Armen hatte, habe ich das auch gemacht, meist mit meinem Vater.

Als ich dann später meine erste Wohnung gehabt habe, so mit 21, da habe ich immer gedacht, dass ich auch jemanden brauche, mit dem ich die Wäsche so schütteln und hängen kann. Aber ich hatte nur eine kleine Wohnung und in dem Haus gab es keinen Trockenkeller mit stramm gespannten Leinen. So habe ich mir ein System ausgedacht, wie ich die großen Betttücher und Laken auf dem kleinen Wäscheständer, den ich hatte, auch trocken bekommen könnte. Dieses Waschen und Putzen war für uns in der Familie immer eine Art Ritual. Das sehe ich jetzt so. Damals wurde das natürlich nicht so gesehen, es war eine Notwendigkeit: Sauberkeit und Hygiene. Mir ist auch einmal der Gedanke gekommen, dass diese Betonung der Sauberkeit und des Putzens, die man meinen Eltern beigebracht hatte und die ich so ganz automatisch übernommen habe,

70

eine unbewusste Reaktion auf das Schuldbewusstsein der Kriegsgeneration war, also der Generation der Eltern meiner Eltern. Es kann auch sein, dass das falsch ist. Vielleicht war es auch einfach das Echo von Robert Koch und der Tatsache geschuldet, dass in unserer Familie viele im Medizinbereich arbeiteten.

Aber zurück zu der Zahl der Wäscheständer. Sie haben ja schon gemerkt, dass ich gerne rechne *(schmunzelt)*. Ich bin jetzt 36. Wenn ich einmal die in meiner Kindheit gehängte Wäsche nicht mitrechne, dann habe ich seit meinem 21. Lebensjahr in der Regel jede Woche so zwei oder drei von diesen Wäscheständern mit 10 Meter Schnur- bzw. Stangenlänge behängt. Also rechnen wir mal konservativ 2,5 pro Woche. Das sind dann im Jahr 130. In 15 Jahren sind das also 1.950. Das ist gar nicht einmal eine so große Zahl, vor allem wenn man das auf 15 Jahre rechnet. Und da ist mir der Gedanke gekommen, dass es vielleicht doch einmal ein klasse Projekt sein könnte, wenn man einfach einmal eine wirklich große Zahl, eine beeindruckende Zahl von Wäscheständern aufstellt, eine richtig große Fläche sollten die einnehmen, ganz viele Wäscheständer. Hunderttausend ist zum Beispiel eine so beeindruckende Zahl. Und dann wollte ich eine Zahl die auch interessant ist. Und, für die Aufstellung der Ständer wäre es ja vielleicht auch gut, wenn das glatt aufgeht mit der Anzahl der Ständer in einer Reihe und der Anzahl der Reihen. Und so bin ich nach einigem Ausprobieren dann auf 142.129 gekommen. Ich war lange erst bei 125.000 weil 125 für mich auch eine zentrale Zahl ist. Es gibt eine ganze Reihe von Serien von mir, die mit der 125 spielen. 125 Variationen von Gelb, Komposition aus 125 Quadraten, 125 Bilder aus der Zukunft. Das ist eine ganze Serie. Ich mag die Zahl 125. Wenn man die Ziffern hintereinander ausspricht, denkt man nach der zwei, dass die drei kommt, so eins, zwei, drei. Aber es kommt die fünf und das ist ein Sprung. Spannend, nur eine Kleinigkeit, aber spannend. Diese Art von Kleinigkeiten, die finde ich faszinierend. Doch für dieses Projekt klappt das nicht mit 125. Die Quadratwurzel von 125.000 geht nicht glatt auf. Das ist 353,55339059327376220042218105242 und so weiter. Bei 142.129 ist die Wurzel 377. Das ist eine schöne Zahl. Und dann habe ich angefangen damit herumzuspielen, mit dieser Zahl und irgendwann war ich mir dann sicher, dass es diese 142.129 Wäscheständer sein müssen."

*[Gespräch mit Markus Laatz auf der Konferenz „Zukunft X2" am 24.11.2018 in Bonn.]*

## _ unvorstellbar

„Nevada. Ich weiß nicht einmal wirklich, ob jeder, der das Wort Nevada hört, in Europa meine ich, sofort an Las Vegas denkt. Das kann ich gar nicht sagen. Meine erste Assoziation bei Nevada ist Wüste und Atomtestgelände. Das ist schon ein ganz vehementer Einschnitt in der Menschheitsgeschichte. Da wurde zum ersten Mal eine Atomexplosion ausgelöst. So viel so schnell freigesetzte Energie. Zerstörerisch. Ein Höllenfeuer auf der Erde, angefacht von den klügsten Leuten ihrer Zeit. Zumindest hielten sie sich für die klügsten Leute, damals. Heisenberg zum Beispiel. Auch, dass man die Forschung dazu hin arbeitsteilig gemacht hat. Da ist das Projektmanagement entstanden. Also ganz viel Intelligenz, eingesetzt für eine fürchterliche Zerstörung. Die gigantische Explosion natürlich, und dann strahlt das noch für Generationen. Eigentlich unvorstellbar. Auch die vielen giftigen Substanzen, die da entstehen.

Jetzt kann man ja sagen, in der Wüste, da ist doch nichts, aber das stimmt nicht. Da sind nur keine Menschen, und das ist für das Militär, für die Leute, die solche Schwereinereien machen wollen, die dafür Zeit und Kapazität brauchen, natürlich ein Anziehungspunkt. Die haben da ein Gelände, ein riesiges Gelände, auf dem die die Welt untergehen lassen können. Und deshalb, finde ich, muss in ein solches Gelände die Kunst gehen. Also ich meine jetzt nicht, dass ich mit den Wäscheständern in das Atomtestgelände gehen will für die Installation. Das ist Quatsch. Ich will ja nicht, dass jemand verstrahlt wird. Aber ich denke, die Kunst muss in die Wüste gehen, in diese Gebiete, von denen man meint, dass sie leer sind, in die Räume wo die aufgeklärte zivilisierte Gesellschaft, die ein Konzept einer Ethik der Verantwortung entwickelt hat, das wir ja alle kennen, nicht präsent ist. Die Kunst muss sagen, dass es diesen Nicht-Raum, der Raum wo das eigentlich Unerlaubte dann doch gemacht werden kann, nicht gibt. Das ist nur so ein Gedanke, einfach dahingesagt. Das ist jetzt nicht ein Konzept oder ein Manifest oder so etwas. Einfach so eine spontane Idee, und vor allem bitte nicht pathetisch verstehen."

*[Michael Holst im Gespräch mit Markus Laatz auf der Konferenz „Zukunft X" am 24.11.2018 in Bonn.]*

## _ immer wieder dupliziert

„Ich habe ganz am Anfang versucht, mir einen Überblick zu schaffen, einfach durch Duplizierung. Ich arbeite ja gerne mit dem Computer. Für die Entwicklung meiner Photographien ist er ja sowieso schon lange das bevorzugte Instrument und die Planung von Projekten, das ist ja eigentlich das, wofür man den Computer ursprünglich einmal eingesetzt hat, als Rechenmaschine. Wahrscheinlich kennt jeder noch aus der Schule die Sache mit dem Quadrieren. Da kommt man sehr schnell auf große Zahlen, wenn man einfach immer das Ergebnis dupliziert. Das kann man in einem Grafikprogramm auch wunderbar machen und so habe ich einfach die erste Zeichnung von einem Wäscheständer, die ich einmal so schnell gemacht habe, immer wieder dupliziert. Ganz schnell war der Bildschirm voll. Dann kann man natürlich den Zoomfaktor verkleinern und man hat wieder Platz. Aber schon ganz schnell werden die duplizierten Wäscheständer immer kleiner und man hat nur noch ein Pünktchen."

[Michael Holst auf der Contemp-Art in Düsseldorf im Januar 1999 im Gespräch mit Gudrun Hilterkamp.]


## _ berechnen

„Stellt man die Wäscheständer wirklich Stoß auf Stoß, dann braucht ein Ständer in der Breite 103 cm. Bei 377 Ständern für eine Reihe sind das also 388,31 Meter. Das wäre also die minimale Kantenlänge für die Aufstellungsfläche. Ich denke wir werden da etwas mehr Spiel einplanen. Da sollten schon so 5 bis 6 Zentimeter auf jeder Seite Platz sein. Der Abstand zwischen den Stangen eines Ständers beträgt immer 6 Zentimeter, von daher denke ich, ist das auch eine gute Zahl für den Abstand zwischen den Ständern. Das sind dann 1,15 Meter für jeden Ständer und 433,55 Meter für die Länge der vorderen Kante der Aufstellungsfläche."

[Michael Holst bei der Vorstellung des Projektes in der Akademie der Künste, Wien, im Januar 2014.]


## _ möglichkeiten

„Es gibt natürlich ganz verschiedene Möglichkeiten die 142.129 Wäscheständer aufzustellen. Wichtig war mir schon, dass es glatt aufgeht, also in jeder Reihe gleich viel

Ständer stehen. Da die Zahl ja nicht durch zwei teilbar ist, gibt es gar nicht so viele Möglichkeiten.“



## _ linie

„Sicherlich hat es etwas, wenn man die Ständer in einer langen Linie aufstellt. Ich denke aber, für dieses Projekt ist eine quadratische Aufstellung wahrscheinlich das Beste. Das hat ästhetische Gründe, aber auch ganz pragmatische. Es ist einfach wesentlich einfacher, für die Aufstellung ein kompaktes quadratisches Gelände zu finden, als eine viele Kilometer lange und nur wenige Meter breite Fläche.“



## _ zeichnen

„Ich habe mir dann einmal einen ganz normalen A4 Bogen genommen und habe angefangen, darauf kleine Rechtecke, so sechseinhalb mal fünf Millimeter, zu zeichnen. – Das habe ich nachher erst ausgemessen. Als ich damit angefangen habe, habe ich mir über die Größe keine Gedanken gemacht, das war einfach die Größe, von der ich dachte, dass sie für eine Testzeichnung, für ein Ausprobieren, gut wäre. – Ich wollte eine Reihe zeichnen mit 377 Rechtecken, die für die erste Reihe der 142.129 Wäscheständer stehen sollten. Das hat natürlich nicht auf das eine A4 Blatt gepasst, auch mit den kleinen Rechtecken nicht, und deshalb habe ich einfach immer noch ein Blatt dazugelegt, wenn ich am Blattrand war. Es sind schließlich 14 Bögen geworden. In den folgenden Tagen habe ich, zunächst auf die vorhandenen 14 Bögen, dann auch auf weitere Blätter, die ich immer dazu gelegt habe, die anderen Reihen gezeichnet. Es war schon eine verrückte Idee, das zu machen und ich habe mir, während ich da im Atelier auf dem Boden lag und diese kleinen Rechtecke zeichnete, ganz oft gedacht, dass ich jetzt aufhöre. Es war ja eigentlich völlig sinnlos wirklich 142.129 Quadrate auf A4 Bögen zu zeichnen. Aber ich habe es doch gemacht. Schließlich sind es 10 Reihen von A4 Blätter geworden, insgesamt 140 Blätter. Die hängen jetzt an einer Wand in meinem Atelier.“

*[Michael Holst im Mai 2017 zu Gast bei Johannes von Lornze im Uhr-Interview der Woche.]*

## _ quadratisch

„Das Seltsame ist, dass ich für die Aufstellungsfläche immer in quadratischen Formen gedacht habe. Das sieht man auch bei den ersten Zeichnungen. Die Rechtecke, die die Wäscheständer symbolisieren, sind etwas kleiner als sieben mal fünf Millimeter, also schon ein Rechteck, aber die wirkliche Proportion ist 103 zu 58 Zentimeter, also eher 1 zu 2. Bei den Zeichnungen habe ich ganz intuitiv zwischen den einzelnen Reihen mehr Platz gelassen, als zwischen den in einer Reihe stehenden Wäscheständern. Wenn man die Ständer nach allen Seiten immer mit dem gleichen Abstand stellt, bekommt man eine Fläche, die genau die Proportion eines einzelnen Ständers hat, also einen riesigen Wäscheständer, und das ist kein Quadrat.“

*[Michael Holst im Juli 2017 im Gespräch mit Johannes Freitag, Münchener Kunstzeitung.]*

## _ vorstellungen

„Irgendwann stellt man dann den ersten Ständer auf, in der Wüste von Nevada. Und dann steht er da. – So stelle ich mir das vor. Und ich denke, das wird ein klasse Gefühl sein, anzufangen mit diesem Projekt, nicht nur in der Theorie, sondern es dann praktisch zu machen, so wie in all den vielen Jahren vorher geplant. Ich glaube das wird ein großartiger Augenblick, wenn der erste Wäscheständer aus dem Karton geholt wird und dann steht er da an dem Platz, der sein Platz ist, in der Installation, der erste Ständer in der ersten Reihe. 376 Wäscheständer werden neben ihm stehen und hinter ihm wird es 376 Reihen geben, wenn alle Ständer aufgestellt sind. 377 Ständer in einer Reihe und 377 Reihen. Das hört sich gar nicht so viel an, 377, aber das sind 142.129 Wäscheständer. Das ist faszinierend."

*[Michael Holst auf der Contemp-Art in Düsseldorf im Januar 1999 im Gespräch mit Gudrun Hilterkamp.]*


## _ trocknen

„Ja, wieviel Wäsche kann man an einem Tag auf den 142.129 Wäschsteständern trocknen, wenn Sie in der Wüste von Nevada stehen? – Die Frage lässt sich ganz unterschiedlich beantworten. Es hängt auch mit der Art der Aufstellung zusammen. Wenn man die Ständer so stellt, dass jeder Ständer durch einen kleinen Pfad zugänglich ist, kann da wirklich ein Mensch hingehen, mit einem Korb, in dem er seine gewaschene Wäsche hat und kann sie zum Trocknen aufhängen. Wahrscheinlich wird sie schon nach einer halben Stunde trocken sein, denke ich mal, bei 40°C und

8 Prozent Luftfeuchtigkeit. Aber das müsste man mal wirklich berechnen."

[Michael Holst auf eine Publikumsfrage bei einer Diskussionsveranstaltung im Kölner „Theater der Kellner", am 25.07.2011.]

## _ berührend

„Das Erstaunliche ist, dass eigentlich alle Dinge eine Poesie entwickeln können. Das ist natürlich eine sehr gewagte Aussage und vielleicht kommen jetzt ganz viele Leute auf den Gedanken, mir Dinge zu schicken, die ganz und gar unpoetisch sind, also das bitte jetzt nicht. Aber ich möchte wirklich jeden einladen, sich einfach einmal in seinem ganz normalen Alltag ein kleines Zeitfenster zu nehmen, und wenn es nur fünf oder zehn Minuten sind, und sich einfach einmal eines der Dinge anzuschauen, die da in dem Raum, an dem Ort sind, da wo er sich gerade befindet. Und es ist ganz erstaunlich, was man da sehen kann. Es kann ein kleiner Kratzer sein, an der seitlichen Fläche eines Schrankes, der eine besondere Form hat, oder eine Lichtreflexion auf dem Boden, die ein ganz spezielles Muster wirft. Ich habe einmal auf einer Zugfahrt einen kleinen Film gemacht – das ist ja das Tolle heute, dass man schon mit einer kleinen Kamera, die habe ich immer dabei, ganz professionelles Filmmaterial produzieren kann –, und da habe ich aufgenommen, wie auf diesem an sich gar nicht inspirierenden fleckigen Grau des Bodens das Sonnenlicht durch die Fenster des fahrenden Zuges fiel und sich das immer veränderte, in einem Rhythmus und mit einer Schwingung, die wirklich poetisch war. Das können dann ganz berührende Momente werden, wenn man sich darauf einlässt, darauf einlassen kann. Also das ist meine Empfehlung, das einfach einmal auszuprobieren. Die meisten Leute, mit denen ich dann nachher gesprochen habe, nach einiger Zeit, die haben mir gesagt, dass sie das dann regelmäßig machen, nicht nur in einer Ausstellung, sondern auch zu Hause und das finde ich klasse. Da kann Kunst etwas verändern."

*[Michael Holst im Gespräch mit Armin Günther auf dem Podium der Art Experimental Basel am 22.17.2014.]*


## _ fläche

„Alltagsgegenstände können eine beeindruckende Wirkung haben. Das kommt natürlich auf den Blick an, aber den soll ein Künstler ja schulen, seinen eigenen und den der Betrachter. Ein Wäscheständer zum Beispiel. Ich habe das einmal nachgemessen, so mit etwas Spiel braucht der 0,7 mal 1,1 Meter Stellfläche, so wie er bei mir im Atelier steht, in einer Ecke. Ich trockne darauf meine Geschirrtücher. Jetzt kann man sich natürlich fragen, wie viel Wäscheständer gibt es auf dieser Welt? Zum Beispiel von diesem Modell und dann, wie viel Platz nehmen die ein, wenn man sie aufstellt? Sie sind ja alle irgendwo aufgestellt, in der Regel. Bei den 142.129 Wäscheständern ist das eine Fläche von 263,90 mal 414,7 Metern, also 109.439,33 Quadratmeter. Die Oberfläche der Erde sind 510.100.000 km2. Also könnte man die Installation, so theoretisch, mehr als viereinhalb Millionen mal auf der Erdoberfläche aufstellen. *(lacht)* Also wenn ich das einmal in Nevada mache, da bleibt noch genug Platz für all die anderen Dinge, die man aufstellen will oder muss."

*[Michael Holst im November 2001 im Gespräch mit Gero Hassler von der Norddeutschen Kunstzeitung.]*

## _ mond

„Kunst ist ja immer auch eine Marke, die der Mensch setzt, ein Zeichen. Durch die ersten Höhlenmalereien wissen wir: Da waren Menschen. Die haben nachgedacht, reflektiert, über ihr Leben, über ihre Stellung in und zur Welt, über die Stellung zu den Tieren und den Sternen und auch zueinander. Das ist Kunst. Das ist ganz interessant, dass man bei einigen Höhlenzeichnungen, bei diesen so extrem frühen Kunstwerken, auch das auf eine bestimmte Konstellation am Himmel oder auch auf Tiere und Witterung, von der man weiß, dass sie damals prägend war, schließen kann. Und ich finde, das prägt die Kunst bis heute. Für mich ist das immer eine Auseinandersetzung. Und wenn ich diese 142.129 Wäscheständer aufstelle, dann heißt das auch: Ich markiere diese Fläche, zeichne sie aus, mache daraus einen Ort, der ein Ort der Kunst ist, ja, und das heißt auch, ich beanspruche diesen Ort, diese Fläche, diesen Raum. Ich will ihn nutzen für dieses Projekt, und ich melde damit auch meinen Anspruch an. Aber es ist natürlich auch eine Einladung, eine zum Herkommen und Hinschauen. Das funktioniert selbst aus dem Weltraum. Die Installation wird auch vom Mond aus sichtbar sein, nicht wirklich groß, aber man wird sie mit bloßem Auge sehen können."

*[Michael Holst am 6. Dezember 2014 im Interview der Woche des Rundfunks Berlin Brandenburg auf eine Frage von Ludwig Roland.]*


## _ verändern

„Das schöne ist, dass man die Wirkung, die die Installation haben wird, nicht simulieren kann. Das muss man einfach auf sich zukommen lassen, das passiert. Und da sind dann ja auch ganz viele Faktoren, die wirken: das Licht, der Wind, vielleicht auch einmal Regen, in jedem Fall der Tau

80

der Nacht, der am Metall der Ständer kondensieren wird. Und dann kommt es natürlich auch immer auf den Blick an, mit dem man sich so einer Installation nähert. Und das ist ja gerade der Gedanke eines solchen Projektes, den Blick zu schulen, zu sensibilisieren. Dann kann man sich darauf einlassen, kann das, was da ist, etwas machen lassen, mit einem. Das ist ein interaktiver Prozess. Die Kunst entsteht erst durch das Betrachten. Das ist bei mir auch so. Ich mache etwas und erst wenn ich es lange angeschaut habe, weiß ich, dass es gut ist, dass ich es herausgeben kann, oder auch nicht. Ganz viele Zeichnungen zum Beispiel, die landen alle in der Mülltonne bei mir, einfach weil ich, und das kann nach ein paar Tagen noch sein, sehe, dass sie mir nichts sagen, dass da bei mir nichts resoniert. Ich bin da sozusagen der erste Betrachter meiner Kunst, und wenn es funktioniert hat, bei mir, dann denke ich, dass es auch bei einem anderen Menschen funktioniert. Das ist auch das, weshalb mir Ausstellungen und Projekte wie diese Installation so wichtig sind. Es geht um den Dialog. Das ist etwas zutiefst menschliches. Vielleicht geht auch in unserer Gesellschaft so viel schief, weil dieser Dialog, dieses miteinander sprechen, nicht mehr stattfindet oder nicht mehr so, wie der Mensch, wie die Gesellschaft es eigentlich braucht. Und das möchte ich verändern. Das ist, so ganz grundsätzlich gesehen, meine Motivation so ein Projekt zu machen.“

*[Michael Holst im August 2016 im Mittagsfunk des Hessischen Landessenders im Gespräch mit Silvie Kling.]*


## _ vierzig grad

„Was eine wirkliche Herausforderung ist, ist das Rollout. Normalerweise werden die Ständer einzeln in Folie eingeschweißt geliefert. Wir haben aber überlegt, dass es besser ist, wenn sie in Kartons verpackt werden, und einfach eine Pappe zwischen die Ständer gelegt wird, als Schutz vor Verkratzung. Das sollte reichen. Die Frage war dann auch, wie viele Ständer in einen Karton gepackt werden sollten. So 30 kg können zwei Personen gut bewegen, das ist eine Erfahrung von anderen Projekten, deshalb sind wir bei 13 Ständern pro Karton gelandet, bei unseren Überlegungen. Ein Ständer wiegt 2,2 kg. Dreizehn Ständern wiegen dann 28,6 kg, dazu noch das Gewicht des Kartons. Das sind dann für die 142.129 Ständer genau 10.933 Kisten. Ich finde das schön, dass in jeder Kiste die gleiche Zahl von Ständern ist, das ist ja auch ein ästhetisches Projekt.

Und dann ist die Frage, wie man die Aufstellung so organisiert, dass die Ständer gleichmäßig stehen und dass auf dem Boden keine Spuren von Fahrzeugen oder von den Leuten sind, die die Ständer aufstellen. Wir haben rollbare Plattformen konstruiert, die die Helfer, die die Ständer aufstellen, immer mit Nachschub versorgen. Die haben dann auch immer Harken und Besen dabei, um den Boden gleichmäßig zu machen, bevor der nächste Ständer aufgestellt wird. Eigentlich ist das ja keine schwierige Sache, so einen Wäscheständer aufzustellen, aber bei Temperaturen von bis zu 40° im Schatten und wenn man das den ganzen Tag macht, dann ist das schon eine Herausforderung."



## _ lange leine

„Manchmal denke ich, es müssten auch gar nicht 142.129 Wäscheständer sein. Es könnte auch einfach eine ganz lange Wäscheleine gespannt werden. Das wären dann 1.421.290 Meter. Die könnte man dann mehr als 35 mal um den Äquator wickeln. Aber ich denke da eher an den Innenhof des Heidelberger Schlosses. Zum Beispiel bei den Schlossfestspielen. Auf der Bühne steht Lady Macbeth, vor ihr eine Schüssel. Sie versucht, ihre blutigen Hände rein zu waschen. Schnell färbt sich die Seifenlauge tief rot. Lady Macbeth greift hastig nach einem Handtuch, immer wieder greift sie nach neuen Handtüchern. Blut ist in den Handtüchern. Sie schreit, wirft die Handtücher auf den Boden. Immer wieder versucht sie ihre Hände rein zu waschen, vergeblich. Immer mehr blutverschmierte Handtücher liegen auf dem Boden.

Zunächst eine, dann immer mehr, schließlich ein ganzes Heer von Wäscherinnen kommt auf die Bühne und sammelt die Handtücher auf, wäscht sie in großen Zubern, die von kräftigen Gestalten herbeigeschleppt werden. Der ganze Schlosshof ist voll von Menschen, die Wäsche waschen, wringen. Leinen werden gespannt, quer über den Schlosshof, von links nach rechts, von oben nach unten. Am Anfang werden die Leinen noch sorgfältig parallel gezogen. Dann werden die Wäscherinnen immer hektischer. Der Platz reicht nicht, Die Leinen werden über- und untereinander gezogen, sie kreuzen sich, schon bald durchspannt ein immer undurchdringlicher werdendes Geflecht von Wäscheleinen den Innenhof des Schlosses. Die aufgehängten Handtücher flattern im Wind. Aus den Handtüchern quillt Blut. Lady Macbeth rennt schreiend durch die Installation von Wäscheleinen, Handtüchern und waschenden Menschen. – Das ist dann jetzt schon eher filmisch gedacht. – Irgendwann würde Lady Macbeth auf dem Boden liegen, in einer Lake aus ihr hervorquellenden Blutes und in der Blutlake schwimmen Wesen, die langsam größer werden und man erkennt die Diktatoren der Vergangenheit und die der Gegenwart. Aber ich glaube, das sprengt etwas das, was man in einer Installation machen kann. Vielleicht sollte ich daraus mal einen kleinen Kurzfilm machen *(lacht)*.“

*[Michael Holst im September 2018 bei den Hirschberger Kamingesprächen auf die Frage, ob es denn nicht auch eine Alternative zu den Wäscheständern gäbe.]*

## _ eng an eng

„Es gab auch die Überlegung, die Installation im Spiegelsaal des Schlosses von Versailles zu machen. Das ist natürlich ein klasse Ort, auch schon aufgrund seiner Historie. Und vielleicht sollte man da auch einmal etwas machen. Das Problem ist, dass da die 142.129 Wäscheständer einfach nicht hineinpassen, zumindest ausgeklappt und nebeneinander gestellt. Der Saal hat eine Fläche von so um die 370 Quadratmeter. Das ist natürlich riesig für einen Saal und durch die Spiegel wirkt er gleich doppelt so groß. Eine wirklich innovative Idee, auch heute noch, und die hat viele Nachahmer gefunden. Wobei man sich das erst einmal leisten können musste, so viele Spiegel zu installieren. Aber für die Wäscheständerinstallation brauchen wir, wenn wir sie eng an eng stellen, eine Fläche von 230 mal 400 Metern. Das sind einfach Dimensionen, die ein klassischer Innenraum nicht leisten kann. Das sind so 14 Fußballfelder.“

*[Michael Holst beim Besuch des Elysee Palastes im Februar 2015.]*

## _ frühstückstraum

„Ich denke, am Abend vor dem Projektbeginn werde ich die Wäscheständer noch einmal durchzählen und auch die Wäscheklammern. Das ist so ein Traum, den ich habe, so ab und zu. Es ist, sie werden lachen, ein Alptraum. 142.129 Wäscheständer zählen und dann dazu die Wäscheklammern und das am Abend vor der Installation. Sie sind noch in den Packungen, die Wäscheklammern, und ich sage mir, im Traum, dass man sich darauf verlassen kann, dass immer 1000 in einem Paket sind, in diesem eincellophannierten Block zusammengepackter Klammern und dann fange ich doch an, sie auszupacken – das muss ja sowieso gemacht werden, denke ich, so zur Rechtfertigung –, und ich beginne sie zu zählen. Es wird eine Katastrophe, denke ich, im Traum, und dann auch noch eine ganze Weile in der Wirklichkeit, wenn ich aufwache, mitten in der Nacht und noch nicht genau weiß, ob ich noch im Traum bin oder schon in der Wirklichkeit. Ich werde das nicht machen, denke ich, und natürlich würde ich die Klammern nicht von Hand nachzählen, einen Tag vor dem Projekt, obwohl ich schon sehr akribisch bin *(lacht)*. Wenn ich dann am Frühstückstisch sitze, am Morgen nach so einem Traum, dann denke ich: Du packst die Wäscheklammern natürlich nicht vorher aus und du zählst sie auch nicht nach, aber dieses Projekt, das wirst du machen, ganz sicher."

*[Michael Holst im Gespräch mit der Zeitschrift artif. Interview in der Ausgabe 4.2002, Seite 54.]*

## _ verlassen können

„Das mit dem Nachzählen ist so ein Ding. Man kann das ganz einfach ausprobieren. Wenn man ein Muster hat, aus kleinen Kugeln zum Beispiel und die sind immer gleichmäßig angeordnet, dann muss man ja nur nachzählen, wie viele es in einer Reihen sind und wie viele Reihen es sind. Aber ich habe als Kind mir einmal darüber Gedanken gemacht, ob es nicht sein könnte, dass man, wenn man dann wirklich nachzählt, doch auf ein anderes Ergebnis kommt, als mit der Rechnung. Es könnte ja sein, dass in irgendeiner dieser vielen Reihen eine der Kugeln, oder der Kreise, die das Muster machen, fehlt und dann sind es eben nicht die 125.000 die man ausgerechnet hat, sondern ein oder zwei weniger. Das hat also gar nichts mit magischem Denken zu tun oder so. Es geht einfach darum, ob man sich auf etwas, was man durch Denken – das Rechnen ist ja auch eine Form des Denkens, eine sehr abstrakte sogar –, ob man dadurch eine wirklich sichere Erkenntnis bekommen kann. Also deshalb finde ich das interessant.“

[Michael Holst im Magizin Zuit-a-jour 2001; Seite 234.]

## _ choreographie

„Das Ganze ist ja auch eine logistische Herausforderung. Bei den meisten Projekten mache ich ja eine Probe im Atelier. Das wird so jetzt nicht gehen, einfach schon allein wegen der Größe der Fläche, die wir für die Installation brauchen werden. Da müssen wir uns viel mehr auf die Simulationen verlassen. Trotzdem wird die Lagerhalle am Containerbahnhof Eifeltor in Köln aber so etwas wie der zentrale Sammelpunkt sein. Das ist zumindest das von mir favorisierte Modell. Da wird alles zusammengestellt, so dass wir in Nevada einfach nur einen Container nach dem anderen auspacken müssen und dann immer genau das haben, was wir für den Aufbau brauchen. Ich kann mir vorstellen, dass das eine richtige Choreographie werden kann. Das müssen wir aber noch einmal von den Kosten durchrechnen. Es kann auch sein, dass es einfach billiger ist, wenn die Lieferanten alles direkt nach Nevada liefern, die haben da ja auch ihre Möglichkeiten, und dass wir mit dem Team in Nevada dann neben dem Aufstellungsort ein Camp

86

aufbauen, da das ganze Material dort dann angeliefert wird und wir es vor Ort für die Installation vorbereiten."

*[Michale Holst im Gespräch mit Mark t'Haven, auf einer Diskussionsveranstaltung im Rijksmuseum Amsterdam am 12.01.2016.]*


## _ der weg

„Der Landweg in Europa ist ja nur ein kleiner Teil der Stecke, den die Wäscheständer zurücklegen müssen. Das ist Logistik, und Logistik ist heute ein eigenes Studienfach. Der Mensch neigt ja dazu, alles zu professionalisieren. Trotzdem: Die Strecke ist eine Herausforderung und ich stelle mir immer gerne vor, wie es ist, so eine Strecke zu Fuß zu gehen. Das ist ja eigentlich die dem Menschen gemäße Geschwindigkeit. Ich denke, man kann schon so gut 20 km am Tag gehen. Bei den gut 900 km, die das von Blatná nach Rotterdamm sind, wäre das ein ganzer Monat. Das ist schon ein Stück. Jetzt wird das natürlich technisch unterstützt gemacht. Doch manchmal denke ich, dass das für die Installation transportierte Material auch etwas von den Eindrücken aufnimmt, die so auf dem Weg liegen. Aber das ist natürlich Unsinn, auch wenn ich die Vorstellung sehr poetisch finde."

*[Michale Holst im Gespräch mit Mark t'Haven, auf der Diskussionsveranstaltung im Rijksmuseum Amsterdam am 12.01.2016.]*


## _ mitnehmen

„Wie ich mir das Ende der Installation vorstelle? Das ist eine seltsame Frage, jetzt, wo ich nur an das Machen, an das Verwirklichen denke, aber ja, die Frage ist natürlich berechtigt. Ich denke erst einmal, dass es ein Ereignis wird, etwas zu dem man hingeht, über das man spricht. Und ich wünsche mir, dass da eine gute Atmosphäre ist, wenn die Installation steht, dass die Menschen, die da sind und schauen, miteinander ins Gespräch kommen, dass sie sich austauschen, und Erfahrungen machen, intensive Erfahrungen. Das ist ja eine Begegnung, so stelle ich mir das vor, mit einem Alltagsgegenstand und der ist jetzt an einem Ort, wo man ihn sonst nicht findet und dann gleich in einer so großen Zahl und ich denke, das löst schon etwas aus. Und ja, die Frage nach dem Ende. Ich denke das sollte das, was da passiert ist, mitnehmbar machen, dass man diesen Eindruck, diese Erfahrung mit nehmen kann, dass man sie teilen kann. Ich glaube, das ist das, was ich mir wünsche, dass es ein Impuls ist."

*[Michale Holst im April 2019 in einem Gespräch mit Jule Treker, New Hamshire Chronical.]*

# 142,129 drying racks in a desert

*Michael Holst about his project*
*"142,129 drying racks in the desert of Nevada"*

## _ meditative

„I do not want to offend anyone, and may be a lot of people will misunderstand that now, possibly, but I think household and housework can be quite meditative. I sometimes even think that, form a certain point of view: I somehow like it, when I do it. So of course it depends on how you do that, how you can do it. And it does not have to be too often. *(laughs)* When you have stress, it's stressful, of course. But okay."

[In conversation with Markus Laatz at the conference „Zukunft X2" on 24.11.2018 in Bonn.]


## _ echos

"Quite classically, on a typical Saturday, I thought about it, hanging up the laundry of the week. I wondered how many drying racks I had already hung with laundry in my life. So as a kid, I've done that from time to time, hanging up the laundry. I thought that was fun. My mother and father went to the basement with a big tub. There, in a room called dry room, hooked on hooks in the wall across the room, lines. As a child, of course, they were infinitely high for me. My father and my mother shook out the big pieces of linen, for example the bed sheets, and pulled them tight so that they would dry on a line. That was something like a right special technique. One took the sheet up, the other down, it was drawn with both hands, which were close together, tight between the two people and then both hands moved at the same time quickly apart from each other. If you did that well, there was a real bang. That was fascinating, that really was an impressive action for me as a kid. Later, the dried linen was removed and shaken once more and pulled tight. There was a lot of movement in the air when the big sheets were shaken and pulled back and forth. When I was a little taller and had enough strength in my arms, I did that too, mostly with my father.

When I later had my first flat, at 21, I always thought that I needed someone to shake and hang my clothes like that. But I had only a small apartment and in the house there was no dry cellar with tightly stretched lines. So I developed a system how to dry the big towels and the bed sheets on the little drying rack that I had. This washing and cleaning was always a kind of ritual for us in the family. I realize that now. Of course it was not seen that way at the time, it was a necessity: cleanliness and hygiene. It occurred to me once again that this emphasis on cleanliness and cleaning, which had been taught to my parents and that I so completely automatically adopted, was an unconscious reaction to the guilty consciousness of the war generation, that is the generation of my parents' parents. It may also be that this is wrong. Maybe it was simply the echo of Robert Koch and the fact that many in our family worked in the medical field.

But back to the number of drying racks. You already may have noticed that I like to calculate *(chuckle)*. I'm 36 years old now. If I do not count the laundry I put on in my childhood, then I usually hang two or three of the drying racks every week. They each have a bar length of ten meters.

I think I did that every week since I was 21 years old. So for a rough calculation we expect 2.5 per week, simply a conservative approach. That's 130 per year and 1,950 in 15 years. That's not even such a big number, especially if you take in account that it is a period of 15 years. And then, at that point, there was the idea that it could be a great project, if you just set up a really big number, an impressive number of drying racks, a number that really can occupy a large, a very large area, quite a lot of drying racks. For example, one hundred thousand is such an impressive number. And then I wanted a number that is interesting too. And, for the erection of the racks, it might also be good if it works out evenly with the number of stands in a row and the number of rows. And so I came to 142,129 after some trial and error. I had, for a long time, 125,000 in my mind, as a number that my fit, simply because 125 is a central figure for me. I have done quite a few series that play with the 125: 125 variations of yellow, composition of 125 squares, 125 images of the future. That's a whole series. I like the number 125. If you pronounce the numbers one after the other, you think after the two that it is the three that has do come, one, two, three. But it is the five, that comes and that's a jump. Exciting, just a small thing, but exciting. This kind of little things are the things that I find fascinating. But this project does not work with 125. The square root of 125,000 does not go smoothly. It is 353,55339059327376220042218105242 and so on. For 142,129, the root is 377. That's a nice number. And then I started playing around with that number and at some point I was sure it had to be these 142,129 drying racks."

[In a conversation with Markus Laatz at the conference "Zukunft X2" on 24.11.2018 in Bonn.]

"Nevada. I really don't know, if anyone who hears the word Nevada, in Europe I mean, immediately thinks of Las Vegas. I can't say that. My first association with Nevada is desert and nuclear testing grounds. Nuclear explosions. That is quite a vehement change in human history. It was the first time that an atomic explosion had been triggered. So much energy released so fast. Destructive. A hellfire on Earth, fueled by the cleverest people of their time. At least they thought they were the cleverest people, at their time. Heisenberg for example. Also, that the research has been based on the division of labour. That's where project management was developed. So much intelligence, used for so much terrible destruction. The gigantic explosion, of course, and then for generations to come: radiation. Actually unimaginable. Also, the many toxic substances that arise there.

Now you can say, in the desert, there's nothing there. But that's not true. There are only no people, and that is of course a magnet for the military, for the people who want to make such a messes, who need time and capacity for it. With the desert, they have a terrain, a huge area where they can let the world go, where they can practice apocalypse. And I think that's why art has to go into such a terrain. So I do not mean that I want to go in the nuclear test area with the laundry racks. I don't want to do the installation there, of course not. That's nonsense. I do not want anyone being contaminated. But I think art has to go to the desert, to those areas that are thought to be empty, to the spaces where the enlightened civilized society, that has developed a concept of an ethics of responsibility, that we all know, is not present. Art has to say that this non-space, this space where the actually interdicted can be done, does not exist.

We, the civilized society, don't allow to give this space a place to be. That's just a thought, just said. This is not a concept or a manifesto or something. Just a spontaneous idea, and above all please do not understand pathetically. "

*[In conversation with Markus Laatz at the conference "Zukunft X" on 24.11.2018 in Bonn.]*

## _ finally small dots

"At the beginning I tried to get an overview, simply by duplication. I like to work with computes. For the development of my photographs, this machine already has been the preferred instrument for a long time and now I use it for planning projects. That actually is what the computer was originally designed for, as a calculating machine. Everyone probably still knows from school the thing about squaring. You can quickly get big numbers just by duplicating the result. You can do that wonderfully in a graphics program, too, and so I simply duplicated the first drawing of a drying rack that I once quickly made as a first try. Very quickly the screen was full. Then you can of course reduce the zoom factor and you have room again. But very quickly, the duplicated drying racks are getting smaller and smaller and you finally have only small dots."

*[At the Contemp Art in Düsseldorf in January 1999 in conversation with Gudrun Hilterkamp.]*

## _ calculating

"If you place the drying racks really push on push, then a rack needs 103 cm in width. At 377 racks for a row, that's 388.31 meters. So that would be the minimum edge length for the installation area. I think we will plan a little more space in between the racks. There finally should be 5 to 6 centimeters on each side. The distance between the racks cords is always 6 centimeters, so I think that's also a good distance between the racks. That's 1.15 meters for each dry- ing rack and 433.55 meters for the length of the front edge of the installation area."

[At the presentation of the project in the Akademie der Künste, Vienna, in January 2014.]


## _ many options

"There are, of course, very different ways to set up the 142,129 drying racks. It was important to me that it works out evenly, so that in each row there will be the same amount of racks. Since the number is not divisible by two, there are not so many options."

[April 2017 in the Jahrhunderthalle in Bochum.]


## _ lines

"Certainly, putting up the racks in a long long line, will have a very special effect, yes. But I think for this project a squared lineup is probably the best. This has aesthetic rea- sons, but also quite pragmatic. It's just a lot easier to find a compact quadratic terrain for the set up than an area many miles long and only a few feet wide."

[Visiting Johannes von Lornze in the Watch-Interview of the week in May 2017]


## _ 140 sheets on a wall

"At a certain point, when ideas already had developed in an quite specific direction, I took a normal A4 sheet and began to draw small rectangles on it, six and a half by five millimeters. – I re measured that later. When I started doing that, I did not worry about the size, it was just the size that I thought would be good for a test drawing, for a try-out. – I wanted to draw a row with 377 rectangles, which should stand for the first row of the 142,129 drying racks. Of course, that did not fit on this one A4 sheet, even with the small rectangles, so I just kept adding a sheet when I was on the bottom of the current page. It has finally become 14 sheets of paper. In the following days, I drew the other rows, first on the existing 14 sheets, then on other sheets that I added. It was a crazy idea to do that, and while I was lying on the floor of the studio drawing these little rectangles, I often thought that I would stop now. It really was completely useless to draw 142,129 squares on A4 sheets. But I did it. Finally, it has become 10 rows of A4 sheets, a total of 140 sheets. They're hanging on a wall of my studio now."

*[Talking with Johannes von Lornze in the Watch-Interview of the week in May 2017.]*

## _ squares

"The strange thing is, that I've always thought of the projects site in square shapes. You can see that just from the first drawings. The rectangles that symbolize the drying racks are a little smaller than seven by five millimeters, so that's a rectangle, yes, but the real proportion is 103 to 58 centimeters, so something near by 1 to 2. In the drawings, I left more space between the rows, as between the drying racks standing in a row. If you always place the drying racks with the same distance on all sides, you get an area that has exactly the proportions of a single drying rack, that is a huge drying rack, and that's not a square."

*[July 2017, interviewed by Johannes Freitag, Münchener Kunstzeitung.]*


## _ greatest moment

"And then, one day, you set up the first drying rack in the Nevada desert. *(smiles with a hardly recognizable shrug)* Yes, and then it stands there. – I imagine it like this. And I think, that's going to be a great feeling, a really great feeling, to start with this project, not just in theory, but to make it practical as it has been planned in all those many years ahead. I think that's going to be a great moment, when the first drying rack is taken out of the box and then it's there in the place that is its place, in the installation, the first rack in the front row. 376 drying racks will stand next to it and behind it there will be 376 ranks, when finally all the racks are set up. 377 racks in a row. That does not sound that much, 377, but that's 142,129 drying racks. That's fascinating, really that is absolutely fantastic. That will be, I think, the greatest moment in my life, up to then. Hope of course, that there will be more great moments following, perhaps even greater moments, but up to then, that will really be the greatest moment, I'm sure, yes."

*[At the Contemp Art in Düsseldorf in January 1999 in conversation with Gudrun Hilterkamp.]*


## _ dry

"Yes, how much laundry can you dry on the 142,129 drying racks in one day when you're in the Nevada desert? – The question may be, depending on assumed preconditions, answered very differently. It also depends on the type of installation. If you place the racks in a way that each drying rack is accessible through a small path, then a person can really go there, with a basket in which the person has its laundry washed and can hang them up to dry. It'll probably be dry after half an hour or less, I guess, at 40° C and 8 percent humidity. But that's only my personnel estimation, you really should calculate that."

*[Answering an audience question at a discussion event in the Cologne "Theater der Kellner", 25.07.2011]*

## _ just give it a try

"The amazing thing is, that actually all things can develop their own sense of poetry. This is of course a very daring statement and maybe many people now come up with the idea of sending me things that are totally unpoetic, so please do not do that now. But I really want to invite everyone to just take a small time window of his normal everyday life, even if only five or ten minutes, and just look at one of the things being are there in the room, in the place where you are right now. And it's amazing what you can see there. It can be a small scratch on the side surface of a cabinet that has a particular shape, or a light reflection on the floor that casts a very special pattern. I myself for example did a little movie some weeks ago on a train ride – that's the great thing about today's cameras, being able to produce quite professional film material, even with a small camera you can do that, I always have one with me – and I filmed the sunlight that was falling through the windows of the moving train and that always changed, in a rhythm and with a vibration that was really poetic. That can become quite touching moments, if you get involved, can get involved in it. So that's my recommendation, just give it a try. Most of the people I talked to afterwards, after some time, told me, that they do it regularly now, not only in an exhibition, but also at home, and I like that. Art can produce change.“

*[In conversation with Armin Günther on the podium of Art Experimental Basel on 22.17.2014]*


## _ four and a half million times

“Everyday objects can have an impressive effect. Of course that depends on the view, but that's what an artist should train, firstly his own and then of course that of the visitors of his exhibitions, that's his job. A drying rack for example. I measured it once. So with some play it has a 0.7 by 1.1 meter footprint, as it stands in my studio, in a corner. I dry my tea towels on it. Of course you can ask yourself, how many drying racks are there in the world. For example, how many from this model and then how much space do they take when you set them up. They are all set up somewhere, I think. For the 142,129 drying racks, this is an area of 263.90 by 414.7 meters, or 109,439.33 square meters. The surface of the earth is round about 510,100,000 square kilometers. So theoretically, you could set up the installation more than four and a half million times on the surface of the earth. *(laughs)* So if I do that for one time in Nevada, there's still room for all the other things you want or need to set up.”

*[In conversation with Gero Hassler of the Norddeutsche Kunstzeitung in November 2001]*

## _ even visible from the moon

"Art is always a mark that man sets, a sign. Through the first cave paintings we know: There were people. They have had thoughts, reflected about their lives, about their position in and to the world, about the relationship to the animals and the stars and also to each other. This is art. This is quite interesting that in some cave drawings, in these extremely early works of art, one can also infer a certain constellation in the sky or even discover animals and weather that one knew ab being formative at that time. And I think that shapes the art to this day. For me it's always an involvement. And when I place these 142,129 drying racks in the desert, that also means: I mark this area, I label it, make it a place that is a place of art, yes, and that also means I claim this place, this area, this space , I want to use it for this project, and I announce my claim. But of course it's also an invitation, one to come and look at. That works even from space. The installation will also be visible from the moon, not really big, but you will be able to see it with the naked eye."

*[December 6, 2014 in the interview of the week of broadcast Berlin Brandenburg answering a question by Ludwig Roland.]*


## _ will to change things

"The nice thing is, that you can't simulate the effect the installation will have. You just have to let it happen, have to let that happen to you. It happens. And then there are quite a lot of factors that will have their effects: the light, the wind, maybe even rain, in any case the dew of the night, which will condense on the metal of the drying racks. And then of course it always depends on the view with which one approaches such an installation. And that is precisely what this project is about: it wants to train the eye, wants to sensitize. Then you can get involved in it, let it do something with you. This is an interactive process. Art first emerges through observation. It's the same with me, too. I do something, a drawing or a painting for example, and only when I have looked at it for a long time, I know that it is good, know that it is ready to be shown to someone else, to an audience, or not. A lot of drawings, for example, end up in the garbage can, simply because I, and this can still be after a few days, see that they do not tell me anything, that for me nothing resonates there. I am, so to speak, the first observer of my artworks, and if it worked with me, I think it works for another person, too. That is also why exhibitions and projects like this installation are so important to me. It's about the dialogue. This is something deeply human. Maybe so many things go wrong in our society, because this dialogue, this talking to each other, no longer takes place or no longer takes place in a way people need it, in a way society actually needs it. And I want to change that. That's my basic motivation to do such a project. That's very simple."

*[August 2016 at the radio station of the Hessian Landessender in conversation with Silvie Kling.]*


## _ a challenge

"The rollout, I think, is a real challenge. Normally, the drying racks are supplied individually shrink-wrapped in foil. But we thought it would be better if they were packed in boxes and simply a cardboard put between the racks to protect them against scratching. That should be enough. The question, then, was how many stands should be packed in a box. So 30 kg very well can be moved by two people, this is an experience of other projects, so we think 13 stands

100

per box will be a good number. A racks' weight is about 2.2 kg. Thirteen racks then, are about 28.6 kg, plus the weight of the box. So if we put 13 in a box that will be exactly 10,933 boxes for the 142,129 racks. I think it's a nice thing, that every box contains the same number of racks, that's also an aesthetic aspect.

And then the question is how to organize the lineup. The racks should be placed even and there should be no traces of vehicles on the ground or footprints of the people setting up the racks. That's important. We've designed rollable platforms that guarantee a steadily supply for the helpers who set up the drying racks. They will have rakes and brooms to make the floor even before the next rack is set up. Actually, that's not a difficult task to set up a drying rack, but at temperatures of up to 40° Celsius and if you do that all day, that's a challenge."

*[With Johannes von Lornze in the Watch-Interview of the week in May 2017.]*

## _ bloody towels on the floor

"Sometimes I think it would not have to be the 142,129 drying racks. It could also be just a very long clothesline stretched. That would be 1,421,290 meters. You could wind it around the equator more than 35 times. But I rather think of the courtyard of Heidelberg Castle, for example at the castle festival. Lady Macbeth is on stage, a bowl in front of her. She tries to clean her bloody hands. Quickly the soapy water turns red, deep red. Lady Macbeth hastily reaches for a towel, again and again she reaches for new towels. Blood is in the towels. She screams, throws the towels on the floor. Again and again she tries to wash her hands clean, but it doesn't work. More and more towels, all full of blood, are lying on the floor.

Washerwomen enter the stage. First one, then more and more, finally a whole army of washerwomen is on the stage. They collect the towels from the ground, wash them in large tubes, which are brought by massive figures. The whole courtyard is full of people who do laundry, who are washing and wringing. Clotheslines are stretched across the castles courtyard, from left to right, from top to bottom. At the beginning the lines are still pulled carefully parallel. Then the washerwomen get more and more hectic. There is not enough space, the lines are pulled over and under each other, they intersect, and soon an increasingly impenetrable network of clotheslines traverses the courtyard of the castle. The towels flutter in the wind. Blood is swelling out of the towels. Lady Macbeth runs screaming through the installation of clotheslines, towels and people washing. – That's already a little bit like a movie. – At some point, Lady Macbeth would lie on the ground, in a spot of blood gushing out of her skirt, and in the steadily growing puddle of blood there are swimming beings, slowly becoming larger and larger. You can recognize the disfigured mad faces of past and present dictators. – I think I have to stop here. That's already something that goes beyond what you can do in an installation. Maybe I should make a short film out of this idea *(laughs with a smile).*"

*[September 2018 at the Hirschberger Fireside Chats, answering the question whether there is an alternative to the drying racks.]*

## _ dimensions a classic interior cannot offer

"We also had the idea of making the installation in the Palace of Versailles, actually in the Hall of Mirrors. This of course is a great place, really fascinating, the history of this impressive monument. And maybe we really should do something there too, an event or an installation. The problem with the 142,129 drying racks is that they just do not fit there, at least if they are unfolded and placed next to each other. The hall has an area of about 370 square meters. This is of course huge for a hall and through the mirror it is twice as big. A really innovative idea, even today. It had found many imitators. It was quite expensive at that time to install so many mirrors and it still is. But for the drying rack installation we need an area of 230 by 400 meters. These are simply dimensions that a classic interior cannot offer. That's 14 football fields."



## _ about counting

"I think, at the evening before the project starts, I will re-count the drying racks and also the clothes pegs. This is one of the dreams I have, from time to time. It is, you will laugh, a nightmare, counting 142,129 drying racks and then the clothes pegs and that at the evening before installation. They're still in the packs, the clothes pegs, and I tell myself, in the dream, that you can trust the manufacturers. There will be the promised 1000 pegs in the unit, counted exactly by a machine. But I still continue to stare at that cellophane block of packed pegs, and then my hand moves and I start unwrapping. It has to be done anyway, I tell myself. That is of course a silly justification, but I already started unwrapping the pegs, and then I start counting. It will be a catastrophe, I think, in the dream, and then for quite a while in reality too, when I wake up in the middle of the night and I do not know exactly, if I am still in the dream or already in reality. I will not do that, I'm saying to myself, and of course I would not recount the pegs by hand one day before the project starts, although I am very meticulous *(laughs)*. When I sit down at the breakfast table on the morning after such a dream, I think: Of course you will not unpack the clothes pegs before the installation starts and of course you will not count them, but you will certainly do this project, you will. "

[Interviewed by journal artif. Interview in issue 4.2002, page 54.]


## _ **uncertain**

"Counting is such a thing, just once again to do a check. You can easily try it. It may confuse you. For example, if you have a pattern of small balls and they are always evenly spaced, you just have to count how many patterns are in a row and how many rows you have. But as a child I once wondered if that could lead you wrong. For example you really count all the objects, and then the result may be different from the result of the calculation. It could be that in one of these many rows one of the balls, or the circles or whatever that makes the pattern, is missing and then it is not the 125,000 that you calculated, but one or two less, or more. So that has nothing to do with magical thinking or anything else stupid stuff. It's just about whether you can rely on your thought, on the processes taking place in your brain. And calculating is a very pure form of thinking, a very abstract one. The question is, if you can get a truly secure knowledge with that. So that's why I find that interesting."

[In the Magizin Zuit-a-jour 2001; Page 234.]

## _ preperations

"The whole thing also is a logistical challenge. For most projects, I'm doing a rehearsal in the studio. We won't be able to do that for this project, just because of the size of the area we will need for the installation. This time we much more have to rely on the simulations. Nevertheless, the warehouse at the Eifeltor container terminal in Cologne will be something like the central collection point. At least that's my favorite model. Everything is put together, so that in Nevada we just have to unpack one container after another and then always have exactly what we need for the construction. I can imagine that this may become a real choreography. But we have to re-calculate this from the costs. It may also be, that it is simply cheaper if the suppliers deliver everything directly to Nevada, they have their special options, and with the team in Nevada we build a camp next to the site and all the material is delivered to that camp, where we can prepare it for the installation."

*[In conversation with Mark t'Haven, at a discussion event at the Rijksmuseum Amsterdam, January 12, 2016.]*

## _ impressions on the way

"The land route in Europe is only a small part of the way, the drying racks have to travel. This is logistics and logistics today is a quite specialized field of study. Man tends to professionalize everything. Still, the track is a challenge and I always like to imagine what it's like to walk that distance. That's actually the natural speed of man, walking. I think you can go as good as 20 km a day. From Blatná to Rotterdam, that is more than 900 km, that would be a whole month. That's really a bit. Now, of course, for the project this is technically supported by engines. But sometimes I think that the material transported for the installation also absorbs some of the impressions that are on the way. But of course that's nonsense, I know that, though I think the idea is a very poetic one."

*[In conversation with Mark t'Haven, at the discussion event at the Rijksmuseum Amsterdam on January 12, 2016.]*

## _ experiences to share

"Do I make up my mind about the end of the installation? That's a strange question, really. Now I am only thinking of doing, of realizing, of making it possible. Yes, but of course it's a question that rises, it's legitimized, yes. — So, first, I think it's going to be an event, something to go to, something to talk about. And I wish there is a good atmosphere, when the installation is working, that the people, who are there and look, talk to each other, that they exchange, and have experiences, intense experiences. This is an encounter with an everyday object, that's my intention, and that is now in a place where you normally can't find these kind of objects and now they are there in such a large number and I think that triggers something. And yes, the question of the final. I think the final should make it possible to take home what happened there, that one can take that impression, that experience; that one can share it. I think, that is what I wish it to be. It should be an impulse. Yes an impulse, that's my wish."

*[April 5, 2019 in an interview with Jule Treker, New Hamshire Chronical.]*

# flusen | fluffs



## _ Schauen

Es gibt Aussagen, die gewagte Aussagen sind. Das mit dem leeren Raum, den es nicht gibt, ist so eine gewagte Aussage, finde ich. Es könnte ihn ja wirklich geben, den leeren, den wirklich ganz und gar leeren Raum, der, vor dem man sich auch fürchten kann, so verstehe ich dieses Diktum vom „horror vacui", das ja in der Kunst sehr viel Wirksamkeit gezeigt hat. Aber gibt es ihn, den wirklich leeren Raum? Gesehen haben kann ihn keiner, denn überall wo wir hinsehen ist etwas, immer.

Es kann ja sein, dass wir das, was wir sehen durch unser Schauen erzeugen, und das halte ich sogar für wahrscheinlich und wenn man das ganz ernst nimmt, müsste das für meine Arbeit als Künstler heißen, dass ich sie nicht mehr tun müsste, tun sollte, vielleicht auch gar nicht mehr tun könnte, denn der Betrachter macht ja die Kunst. Er schafft mit seinem Schauen das was er sieht.

Ich habe diese Vorstellung für eine ganze Zeit als sehr unangenehm empfunden und wenn ich mich hingesetzt habe und eine Ausstellung konzipiert habe, dann hat mich das behindert, ja richtig gelähmt und ich habe wirklich Tage gehabt, da konnte ich überhaupt nicht arbeiten, da ist einfach nichts passiert und erst dann ist mir der Gedanke gekommen, dass ich ja vielleicht ein Begleiter bin für dieses

Schauen und ich schaue ja auch und schaffe damit und ich kann anderen helfen zu sehen und das fand ich dann einen wirklich schönen Gedanken und der treibt mich seitdem das zu machen, was ich mache und was mir so wichtig ist.



## __ Es ist einfach alles Physik

Ich hätte Laplace lesen können oder Descartes, wahrscheinlich hätte ich viel früher Descartes lesen sollen. Der innere stille Glanz, mit der so eine Fluse wandert, auf dem Stoff der Hose zum Beispiel, ist einfach zu bewundern. Das meine ich ganz ehrlich. Da ist so viel Leben in so einem kleinen Stück Materie, soviel Interaktion mit seiner Umgebung, so viel Sensibilität und Empfindlichkeit, auf die Spannungen zum Beispiel, die so ein synthetischer Stoff ausübt, auf eine Baumwollfluse. Das ist natürlich alles Physik und so weiter, es ist aber auch einfach ganz wunderbar. Und mir ist es wichtig das zu sehen.



## __ Boston

Boston ist eine Herausforderung. Das war mein erster Gedanke, als das Angebot kam. Ich habe natürlich sofort Ja gesagt. Aber mir war auch sofort klar, dass das eine wirkliche Herausforderung werden würde. Die Installationen in Zürich und Basel, selbst die in Frankfurt, die ja schon fast so viele Quadratmeter hatte, wie die in Boston, das war alles irgendwie noch handhabbar, der Aufwand schon ganz erheblich, aber noch in dem Bereich mit dem das Team Erfahrung hatte. Natürlich wollten wir es in Boston auch ganz besonders gut machen. Die Voraussetzungen dort, allein von den Räumlichkeiten, sind einfach ideal. Und deshalb haben wir uns auch gleich daran gesetzt.

Ganz wichtig war mir, dass, so wie bei den anderen Installationen auch, der interaktive Audio-Guide auf die Räume abgestimmt wird. Das ist nicht trivial. Wir haben allein drei Tage die Akustik der Räume vermessen. Das Datenmodell ist mehr als 3 Terrabyte groß. Und dann hatten wir ein Problem mit den Trackern und den Frequenzen für die Übertragung auf die Headsets. Das ist ja eigentlich alles standardisierte Technik. Aber die Frequenzbänder, die wir dafür bei den bisherigen Projekten in Europa genutzt hatten, durften wir in Amerika nicht nutzen. Da sind die Bänder anders zugeteilt. Eigentlich kein Problem, dachten wir. Die Bandbreite war sogar etwas größer, nur mit der Reichweite gab es ein Problem, wegen der anderen Frequenz. Wir brauchen praktisch doppelt so viele Repeater, was auch mit der soliden Konstruktion des Boston Conference Center zusammenhängt. Das ist von 1920 und die haben da jede Menge Stahl verbaut. Als freie Träger, sehr massiv und auch in dem Beton. Und das hat ganz interessante Effekte. Meistens schluckt es die elektromagnetischen Wellen. Manchmal leitet es sie aber auch um und verstärkt sie sogar, und da muss man wirklich jeden Punkt ausmessen, damit das System dann zuverlässig funktioniert.

Als wir das dann stehen hatten, haben wir gemerkt, dass es in einigen Räumen eine Überlagerung mit den elektrischen Feldern gab, die wir nutzen um die Flusen zu steuern. Und das ließ sich nicht einfach umstellen, weil, so eine Fluse ist ja nicht wirklich schwer, aber sie braucht ein sehr spezifisches elektrostatisches Feld um zu schweben, so wie wir das ausprobiert haben und bei den bisherigen Projekten hat das ja auch prima geklappt. Doch jetzt mussten wir das völlig neu machen und das in drei Tagen, ein System, für das wir ein halbes Jahr gebraucht haben, um es zuverlässig ans Laufen zu bekommen. Das war schon wirklich hart. Aber letztendlich hat es dann doch geklappt und ich bin dem Team einfach wirklich dankbar für die tolle Arbeit. Das war phantastisch.

*[Michael Holst im Januar 2020 im Gespräch mit Julian D. Richardson vom New York Sculpture Magazin]*

von Hans Peter Markstein

# _ „Man begreift es erst wirklich, wenn man schon wieder zu Hause ist."

Kommt man in den großen Hauptsaal des Bostenen Conferen Center an der Baltimore Avenue, einem Funktionsbau aus den 1920er-Jahren, mit großen Tagungssälen, der jetzt, seit einiger Zeit, als Ausstellungszentrum genutzt wird, ist das erste was man denkt: Der Raum ist leer. Und das ist er auch. Ein großer, rechteckiger leerer Raum. Erst nach einer Weile bemerkt man, dass hier doch etwas ist: kleine fast unsichtbare Flusen. Sie liegen auf dem Boden und, das zeigt der zweite, immer noch und zunehmend mehr irritierte Blick, sie finden sich, wenn auch in geringer Zahl, an Wänden und den hoch angebrachten Lüftungsklappen. Dass sie einem auffallen, nach einiger Zeit, hat mit der subtilen Art der Inszenierung zu tun. Wenn man sie einmal bemerkt hat, sieht man, dass sie überall liegen, sich bewegen, ob durch das Umhergehen des ratlosen Betrachters in dieser Installation, in der er ausgestellte Objekte sucht, oder durch einen irgendwoher kommenden Windzug oder vielleicht auch, der Gedanke kommt nach einiger Zeit, durch elektrische Ladung. Sind es Synthetikfasern, die da über den Boden schweben, knapp über dem Boden, hinten in der großen freien Ecke des Raumes, da wo gut eine imposante Skulptur stehen könnte, oder Platz wäre für ein großflächiges Gemälde? Aber da ist nichts dergleichen. Was es gibt, in diesem Raum, dessen Leere immer noch erdrückend ist, sind auf eine sehr geschickte Weise an nicht zu identifizierenden Orten angebrachte Lichtquellen. Sie lassen die Fasern leuchten, für einen kurzen Moment nur, manchmal kaum wahrnehmbar, dann lange deutlich sichtbar, an einer Stelle wo man vielleicht gerade hergegangen ist und dachte, da sei nichts. Doch das ist nicht richtig. Sie sind überall, diese Flusen, diese kleinen Fädchen.

Es sind Fragmente, ist die Assoziation, die sich einstellt, nach einiger Zeit, aus einem Grund der sich nicht erschließt. Und doch bleibt der Gedanke an das Fragmentarische präsent, im Kopf des Betrachters, der durch diese Installation geht und er denkt daran, dass diese kleinen Fädchen vielleicht das Überbleibsel eines abgelegten Kleidungsstücks sein könnten, vielleicht von einer Person, die schon lange nicht mehr lebt oder deren Verbleib unbekannt ist. Was könnte man über diese Person wissen, über ihr Leben, ihre Wünsche und Vorstellungen, wenn man eine dieser Flusen untersuchen würde, so genau wie das heute möglich ist, mit den feinen chemischen Methoden, den Mikroskopen und Massenspektrometern? Gäbe das eine Geschichte und wie wahr wäre sie? Wie wahr könnte sie sein?

An dieser Stelle besteht die Gefahr, sich in tiefsinnige, abgründige oder auch grenzenlos phantastische Gedanken zu verlieren. Doch das sollte man nicht. Es ist hilfreich, dass es zu dieser Installation einen außergewöhnlich gut gemachten Audio-Guide gibt. Am Eingang bekommt man einen voluminösen Kopfhörer ausgehändigt. Der hat eine ganz erstaunliche Klangqualität, die wohl der eines Referenz-Kopfhörers im Tonstudio entsprechen mag, und er hat zwei kleine, jeweils an der rechten und linken Hörmuschel außen angebrachte Tracker, die die Position des Besuchers im Raum sehr genau an das Audio System weiterleiten. Und so bekommt man, wenn man mit diesem technisch anspruchsvollen Audio-Guide durch die Installation geht, den Klang, die Sprache und die Musik immer genau passend zu der Position im Raum zugespielt, an der man sich gerade befindet. Das ist ein völlig neues Konzept eines Audio-Guides. Ja, eigentlich ist der Begriff Audio-Guide hier auch irreführend. Es ist eine individuelle, interaktiv räumliche Klanginstallation, durch die der Besucher da geht. Und der so präzise die fein abgemischten Klangereignisse wiedergebende Kopfhörer gibt dem Besucher an bestimmten Stellen der Installation ganz unmerklich Impulse, seinen Schritt zu verlangsamen oder zu beschleunigen oder seine Blick- oder Gehrichtung zu ändern. Der Übergang in einen anderen Raum der Installation erfolgt so organisch, ist aber mitunter auch als Bruch oder überraschende Kontrastierung inszeniert.

Da findet man sich plötzlich in einem kalten Raum. Grellweißes Licht aus dem Nirgendwo einer gleichmäßig strahlenden überhoch entfernten Deckenfläche. Er hätte sie auch „Staub" nennen können, diese Installation, hat der Künstler in einem Interview gesagt. Und in diesem Raum hat man wirklich den Eindruck es läge ein feiner Staub in der Luft, sehr gelichmäßig verteilt, mehr spürbar als sichtbar und doch ungeheuer präsent. Da möchte man eine Maske anlegen, denke man schon beim Betreten des Raumes.

„Follow the red line" steht da auf einem Schild, am Raumeingang. Und der Besucher folgt dieser Anweisung. Die rote Linie, sauber auf den glattpolierten Boden aufgeklebt, scheint der Weg zu sein, der offensichtlich einzig erlaubte, der einzig sichere Weg durch diese Gefahr, Gefahrenzone mit den vielen Unwägbarkeiten, die da in dem nicht Sichtbaren des gleichmäßig gefühlten Nebels oder Dunstes liegen.

Ganz anders, luftig und leicht ist die Stimmung des sich anschließenden Raumes. „Galerie" heißt er und der Katalog verspricht Gemälde mit sprechenden Titeln: „Der

See" soll an Wand drei hängen, „Gartenhaus am sonnigen Nachmittag im Schnee" an der Wand gegenüber, so der Katalog. Aber wenn man in dem Raum ist, sieht man nichts. Wieder ein leerer Raum. Nur wenn man ganz genau hin sieht, bemerkt man, dass da einmal Gemälde, genauer große Rahmen, gehangen haben müssen, an diesen Wänden, für einige Zeit und sie haben ihren Schatten hinterlassen auf dem ansonsten so tadellosen Weiß der Wand. An einer Stelle scheint einer der Arbeiter der Ausstellung, einer der mit dem Aufbau Befassten, unvorsichtig gewesen zu sein. Die Spur eines schmutzigen Handschuhs könnte es sein, der diagonal nach unten weisende Streifen links, im unteren Drittel der Wandfläche.

Was macht einen so aufmerksam, wenn man in diesem leeren Raum steht? Hier ist nichts und doch sind im Betrachter so viele Prozesse, so viele Bilder, wie in keiner anderen Installation. Eine erstaunliche Sensibilisierung hat stattgefunden und mit diesem sensibel geschulten Blick kommt man in den nächsten Raum. Der ist voll mit großformatigen Leinwänden. Endlich, denke man. Da ist etwas. Ausstellungsexponate. Etwas von dem man erzählen kann, wenn man gefragt wird, was man gesehen hat, bei diesem Besuch, der doch nun schon über eine Stunde dauert. „Großformate" heißt der Raum. Und sie sind wirklich groß diese Leinwände. 3 Meter mal 4 Meter die kleinste. Die größte, sie füllt die ganze Stirnwand des Raumes, misst 8,90 Meter mal 4,20 Meter. Es sind monochrome Flächen, gut aufgespannte Leinwände, auch die großen tadellos straff gezogen ohne jede Falte oder Wellung und sie sind lackiert, monochrome, meist mit einem leicht gebrochenen Weiß. Ob sie changiert, die auf den Leinwänden aufgetragene Farbe, kann man nicht sagen. Es gibt viele farbliche Nuancierungen, aber das sind wohl Schattenwürfe, ungleichmäßig reflektiertes Licht der Decke und auch der Betrachter, der vor der Leinwand steht, nimmt oder wirft Licht.

Dann fällt einem auf, dass auf dem Lack Flusen sind, größere und kleinere in den unterschiedlichsten Farben. Sie bilden Muster, treten hinter das Weiß der Leinwand, dem sie anhaften, zurück und verschwinden bisweilen ganz, um dann an einer anderen Stelle, ganz unvermutet, wieder hervorzutreten. Das nicht-da-sein, das nicht-mehr oder noch-nicht einer Erscheinung, scheint das zentrale Thema dieser Installation zu sein. Normalerweise haben Flusen auf einer lackierten Fläche nichts zu suchen. Hier passen sie. Sie entspannen das so allgegenwärtige Weiß, lassen es warm, manchmal auch verspielt, in jedem Fall aber heiter erscheinen. Erst durch die Flusen bekommt dieser Raum seine luftig helle Heiterkeit.

Der letzte Raum dieser Installation heißt „Verschwunden". Als wenn nicht schon alles verschwunden wäre, was verschwinden kann, in dieser Ausstellung. Auf dem Boden, wieder dem Boden, sind Schleifspuren. Schwere Kisten sind hier herausgetragen worden. Ein abgesprungener Spanngurt liegt in einer Ecke, ein von einer Holzpalette herausgebrochenes Stück Holz daneben. Von seinem Volumen ist es das größte Exponat der ganzen Installation. Die Arbeiter, die die Sachen hier herausgetragen, geschleppt, über den Boden geschoben haben, trugen grobe Schuhe, sie sind durch Schlamm gegangen. Das sieht man an den Spuren, die sie auf dem Boden hinterlassen haben.

Das Licht, das gleichmäßig von der Decke kommt, in die zu schauen eine angenehme Entspannung ist und ein wirklicher Gegensatz zu den Spuren des Chaos auf dem Boden, lässt einen dann Hoffnung schöpfen. Erst draußen auf dem kleinen Innenhof wird man wieder wirklich ruhig, wenn man auf der Bank sitzt, von der man gar nicht merkt, dass auch sie Teil der Installation ist. Dann blättert man noch einmal durch den Katalog, als Nachklang zu diesem emotional so aufwühlenden Gang durch die leeren Räume und die vielen Millionen Fusseln. Und dann bemerkt man, dass man noch welche von ihnen an den Schuhen hat oder sie sich an einen Teil der Kleidung angeheftet haben. Noch Tage später finde ich an meiner Kleidung, auch auf dem Boden meiner Zimmer und auf den Textilbezügen meiner Möbel diese synthetischen Fusseln mit ihrer intensiv fluoreszierenden Farbe. Sie haben sich mir ganz unbemerkt angeheftet, als ich durch die scheinbar leeren Räume ging. Der Gedanke kommt auf, dass dies wohl die erste Ausstellung eines Künstlers ist, in der es zum Konzept der Ausstellung gehört, dass die Besucher einige der Exponate mit nach Hause nehmen.

# _ENERGIEGELADEN

## _ Leer Räume

*von Yoko Kawakami*

Es ist eine erstaunliche Erfahrung, die die neue Installation von Michael Holst vermittelt. Man steht in diesen leeren Räumen und schaut auf die Wände, aber da ist nichts. Sie sind leer, wirklich völlig leer. Irgendwann versucht man auf dem gleichmäßigen Weiß – die Maler haben ihre Arbeit gut gemacht, denkt man – eine Struktur zu erkennen. Doch da ist keine, da ist gar nichts. Ganz zum Schluss, man wollte gerade schon enttäuscht aus dem Raum gehen, mit einem ein angedeutetes Verständnis suggerierenden Lächeln, das nicht wirklich gelingt, die Enttäuschung vor sich selbst verbergend, weil man nicht zugeben will, dass man nichts gesehen hat, da fällt der beschämte Blick auf den Boden und man sieht eine Struktur, die mit dem eigenen Schatten, dem fliehenden, interagiert, dreht sich um und merkt erst jetzt, dass man die ganz Zeit herumgelaufen ist, in dem Bild, das man gesucht hat, das man seine Spuren in ihm hinterlassen hat, es selbst mitgestaltet hat, so wie die vielen andere Besucher, denn das Bild ist auf dem Boden, ist der Boden und die farbigen Flusen, elektrostatisch aufgeladen, die sich auf ihm hin und her bewegen. Der Boden hat eine spezielle Beschichtung, die elektrostatische Felder unterschiedlicher Intensität erzeugt, Felder die sich verändern und so eine

117

Bewegung erzeugen, die mit der Bewegung der durch den Raum gehenden Besucher interagiert.

Beim Betreten des Raumes haben sich die Flusen an die Schuhsohlen geheftet, und je nachdem, wie die einzelnen Zonen des Bodens präpariert sind, werden sie eingefangen oder wieder abgegeben. Ein beständiger Dialog des sich stetig verändernden Bildes auf dem Boden mit den durch das Bild schreitenden Besuchern. Ich frage mich, wie vielen der Besucher das aufgefallen ist, und wie viele, wie ja auch beinahe ich, einfach mit einer elegant verborgenen Enttäuschung aus dem Raum gegangen sind und vielleicht erst zu Hause bemerkt haben, dass da etwas an ihren Schuhen heften geblieben ist, oder an ihrer Kleidung. Ich bin glücklich, dass ich eine derjenigen bin, die es schon im Raum bemerken konnten, die die Chance hatten, sich noch einmal umzudrehen, mit dem durch die Erkenntnis neu geöffneten Blick und es in sich aufnehmen konnten, dieses Momentum, das die Installation erzeugt.

Eine wirklich erstaunliche Installation, denke ich, und ein wirklich außergewöhnlicher Künstler, der mit den Fußspuren seiner Besucher ein Bild entstehen lässt, das als Geschenk ganz und gar sein Bild ist. Und dann ist die so unerträglich erscheinende Leere plötzlich gefüllt mit einer Poesie, deren ungeheure Intensität mich mit all denjenigen verbindet, die diese Installation besucht haben und noch besuchen werden. Zu sehen aktuell in Boston bis zum 21. April.

*[Dieser Text erschien am 10. Januar 2020 in Ashi Shimbun, Tokio. Übersetzung: Mayamoto Masahiri.]*

## __ Nur Worte

*Helga T. Green:* Wenn man sich über Sie informieren will, im Netz, zum Beispiel, dann findet man nur Worte. Es gibt von Ihnen als Person kein Bild. Sie weigern sich fotografiert zu werden. Warum?

*Michael Holst:* Wenn Sie das in einem Satz beantwortet haben wollen, ganz kurz und knapp, dann ist das, weil ich will, dass mein Werk im Mittelpunkt steht. Ich will nicht, dass es um meine Person geht, es soll um das gehen, was ich mache, als Künstler.

*Helga T. Green:* Sie machen das ja sehr konsequent. Auch zu Ausstellungseröffnungen kommen Sie immer in ganz unterschiedlicher Kleidung, man könnte auch sagen Verkleidung. In Frankfurt waren Sie auch einmal in einem Goethe Kostüm unterwegs.

*Michael Holst:* Kostüm ist nicht richtig. Ich habe das getragen, was man in der Goethezeit trug, als Mann. Das hat natürlich etwas mit Frankfurt zu tun. Wenn man in Frankfurt Kunst macht und sich des Ortes bewusst ist, nicht einfach nur hier etwas macht, was man auch in New York machen könnte oder in Boston oder Sydney, dann hat das natürlich auch mit Goethe zu tun, selbst wenn man sich nicht direkt auf ihn bezieht. Das habe ich ja bisher nie getan. Aber Goethe hat in Frankfurt gelebt, die Stadt hat ihn geprägt und wenn man sich auf eine Stadt einlässt, dann macht sie etwas mit einem. Sie hat etwas mit Goethe gemacht und sie macht etwas mit mir, und da ist es manchmal gut, dass man das auch visuell umsetzt und genau deshalb habe ich damals diese

Kleidung getragen. Die ist übrigens, wenn sie gut gemacht ist, sehr bequem, man kann sich darin durchaus wohl fühlen. Und ich denke, Goethe hat sich auch wohl gefühlt, in der Kleidung die er trug und in der Rolle, die sie, und die Gesellschaft und seine Herkunft, sein Elternhaus, ihm zuwies und die er gestaltet hat, mit der er auch gespielt hat, auch mit ihren Grenzen.

*Helga T. Green:* Es ist aber auch immer eine Verkleidung. Wer Sie auf einer Vernissage erlebt hat, der erkennt Sie auf der anderen nicht unbedingt, und erst recht nicht, wenn er Ihnen auf der Straße begegnet. Als ich Sie das erste Mal getroffen habe, bei einem Pressetermin, da trugen Sie einen Maßanzug, Hemd und Krawatte, heute sitzen Sie mir in einer lässigen Jeans und einem lockeren Pullover gegenüber. Sie sind immer ein Anderer, könnte man denken.

*Michael Holst:* Ich bin schon immer derselbe. *(lacht)* Da habe ich kein Problem. Ich ändere gerne die Erscheinung, auch weil es interessant ist, wie die Menschen darauf reagieren. Das ist ja das was Kunst ausmacht, eine Reaktion bei Menschen zu erzeugen. Ich bin in meiner äußerlichen Erscheinung immer anders, weil es ja auch immer andere Projekte sind, die ich mache. Und die verlangen, anders vorgestellt zu werden. Wie gesagt, es geht um das was ich mache, um die Inhalte meiner Werke. Es geht nicht darum mich als Person zu inszenieren.

*Helga T. Green:* Sie nehmen sich damit aber auch die Möglichkeit eine Marke zu entwickeln. Kann man sich das als Künstler heute noch erlauben? Es gibt nicht einmal ein offizielles Pressefoto von Ihnen.

*Michael Holst:* Ich erlaube mir das, ich mache das einfach. Ja. – Ich bin Künstler. Und als Künstler nehme ich mir die Autonomie, mich meiner Abbildung zu verweigern. Das geht. Und das wird auch akzeptiert.

*Helga T.* Green: Sie haben einmal einen Journalisten verklagt, weil er nach einem Interview, das Sie ihm gegeben haben, ein Bild von Ihnen veröffentlicht hat.

*Michael Holst:* Nein, das ist nicht richtig. Ich habe ihn nicht verklagt. Das war nicht nötig, und es ist auch nicht zur Veröffentlichung gekommen. Die Geschichte wird immer falsch erzählt. Er hat ein Interview, das er mit mir gemacht hat, einer großen Zeitung angeboten, auch mit einem Bild, das er, ich habe das nicht bemerkt, von mir in der Lobby des Hotels, wo wir uns getroffen haben, von einem dafür bezahlten Fotografen, hat machen lassen. Aber die Redaktion der Zeitung hat bei mir im Büro angefragt, ob das Bild den autorisiert sei und das war es natürlich nicht und so wurde das dann nicht veröffentlicht. Ob die Zeitung dann da gerichtlich gegen den Journalisten vorgegangen ist, das kann ich nicht sagen. Von meiner Seite war das damit erledigt.

*Helga T. Green:* Und Sie denken, dass Sie das so durchhalten können oder wollen? Sie sehen doch ganz gut aus, so wie Sie mir jetzt gegenübersitzen. Sie könnten ja auch mal in einer Talkshow auftreten, ich denke das wäre auch für Ihre Kunst gut.

*Michael Holst:* Nein, das wird es nicht geben, Fernsehen und so, nicht einmal meine Stimme in einem Podcast, oder ein Radiointerview. Da bin ich konsequent. Es gibt nur die Buchstaben. Wenn Sie wissen wollen, was ich über meine Kunst denke, wie ich sie erkläre, dann müssen Sie lesen. Mein erster Galerist, so ganz am Anfang, da wollte er mich, wie er sagte, „aufbauen" als Künstler. Und es gibt da ja auch die großen Vorbilder, nicht nur in der Gegenwart. Picasso zum Beispiel, der hat sich, das ist ja bekannt, inszeniert, als Person, da ist der Name wichtiger als das Werk, zumindest hat sich das so entwickelt, und ich denke das wollte er auch. Das ist ja auch okay. Und es ist ja auch eine Leistung, wenn man das so hinbekommt. Aber ich, ich will das nicht. Ich habe da ein anderes Verständnis von Kunst. Kunst muss sich auch wehren, wehren können. Ich mache Bilder, Bilder die in den Köpfen der Menschen entstehen sollen, beim Betrachten, beim Besuchen von Ausstellungen und Installationen, beim Reden, Diskutieren und Nachdenken. Da brauche ich kein Bild von mir als Person. Das steht im Personalausweis. Über mich als Künstler sagt der Personalausweis nichts. Wie gesagt: Wer wissen will, wie ich meine Kunst sehe, der muss lesen. Da gibt es nur die Buchstaben. Das ist doch etwas Wunderbares.

## ___ Flusen

*Helga T. Green:* Hans Peter Markstein, der ja ein wunderbares Essay über Ihr aktuelles Projekt „Flusen" geschrieben hat, hat bei einer Ausstellungseröffnung mit Bildern der Installation, ich glaube es war sogar die Ausstellung in Frankfurt, gesagt, sein Gedanke sei es gewesen, dass Sie für dieses Projekt das Goethekostüm zerfetzt haben, dass die Flusen dieses Kostüm sind, seine Reste, die sich nicht wegspülen lassen, die Spur einer DNA, die zu unserer Kultur gehört, auch wenn wir uns ihrer gar nicht mehr bewusst sind.

*Michael Holst:* Ja, das ist natürlich ein sehr schönes Bild und Hans Peter Markstein schreibt wirklich klasse Texte, er ist jemand, der sich einfühlt in das worüber er schreibt, und der es auch versteht. Und es ist ja, so sehe ich das wirklich, auch einfach ein Zeichen, dass das, was ich da mache, mit meinen Ausstellungen, funktioniert, wenn eine Installation solche Gedanken auslöst. In diesem Fall allerdings, muss ich sagen, dass ich nicht so richtig glücklich bin, mit diesem Bild. Er wollte das auch in das Essay hineinschreiben, also er hatte das da schon stehen, wollt aber mit mir noch einmal darüber sprechen, und das finde ich gut bei ihm, er fragt die Künstler, wenn er etwas hat, wo er sich nicht sicher ist. Das machen andere Journalisten oder Publizisten nicht. Und ich habe ihm gesagt, dass ich das viel zu konkret finde. Als eine Assoziation, so für ihn, wenn er durch die Ausstellung geht, finde ich das völlig okay. Aber so in einem Text, der dann auch noch im Katalog der Ausstellung steht, finde ich das viel zu konkret. Das leitet den Besucher in eine viel zu festgelegte Richtung, macht diese leichten, schwebenden Flusen viel zu bedeutungsschwer. Das will ich nicht. So als Text, ist das einfach falsch. Als flüchtiger Gedanke, der bei jemandem aufkommt, der meine Werke kennt und der vielleicht auch schon einige andere Installationen von mir besucht hat, da ist das okay. Aber in einem Essay, nein, das ist dann einfach doch nicht richtig und ich will auch nicht immer mit dem Goethe Thema verbunden sein, nur weil ich einmal dieses Kostüm getragen habe. Das ist ja schon über zehn Jahre her, und das ist dann auch nicht mehr aktuell.

*Helga T. Green:* Es ist natürlich schwer, wenn man in einem leeren Raum steht und einem dann alle möglichen Gedanken kommen, zu verstehen was der Künstler, der diese Installation konzipiert hat, sich gedacht hat.

*Michael Holst:* Natürlich, aber es geht ja gerade darum, dass in diesem leeren Raum der Raum da ist, für das was in einem ist. Diesen Raum hat man ja heute fast nirgendwo mehr. Es ist ja alles strukturiert, durchgeplant, mit Inhalten und Bezeichnungen gefüllt. Es gibt ja keine leeren Flächen mehr. Über die Erde hat man ein feingliedriges Koordinatensystem gelegt. Jeder Punkt auf ihr hat eine Nummer, also Breitengrad und Längengrad, und selbst der Kosmos ist ausgemessen, noch nicht so genau wie die Erde, aber auch schon erstaunlich genau. Und überall sind Texte und Bilder und Sprache und Geräusche. Da ist ein leerer Raum schon etwas ganz außergewöhnliches. So ist das bei mir entstanden, dieser Gedanke. Und dann der Gedanke, dass da doch etwas ist, immer noch, in diesem leeren Raum. Und das sind die Flusen, diese kleinen Fädchen, die man kaum sieht, die kaum sind, die aber überall sind. Auch weil Sie ja gerade das von Hans Peter Markstein, mit dem zerfetzten Goethekostüm gesagt haben, bin ich da jetzt wirklich vorsichtig selbst so konkrete Bilder zu benennen, aber ich habe da an die Stringtheorie gedacht. Da sind es ja auch diese Strings, man könnte sagen Saiten, oder eben auch kleine Fäden, aus denen die Welt besteht, eben mathematisch beschriebene Fädchen in einem multidimensionalen Raum.

## __ Tracking

*Helga T. Green:* Sie benutzen bei Ihrer Installation viel Technik. Auch wenn das von außen so gar nicht sichtbar ist, hinter dem was man da in den scheinbar leeren Räumen sieht, und über den Kopfhörer auch hört, steckt ein ganzes Arsenal von High-Tech-Gerätschaften. Ein Rezensent der Bostoner Installation hat da kritisch angemerkt, dass man dieser Technik als Besucher hilflos ausgeliefert ist. Weil man sie nicht sieht, kann man sich auch nicht gegen sie wehren.

*Michael Holst:* Ja, das ist richtig und wirklich gut beobachtet. Ich hätte gar nicht erwartet, dass man so etwas im amerikanischen Feuilleton lesen würde. Vielleicht ist es auch deshalb, weil die Installation damit einen Nerv der Gesellschaft trifft: Das wirklich Bedrohliche sieht man nicht. Es steht in einem kleinen Kasten, oder einem Regal aus Metall, in einem Nebenraum, zu dem man keinen Zugang hat. Wenn man wirklich die Ohren spitzen würde, dann könnte man vielleicht das Rauschen der Lüfter hören, oder das Brummen eines Transformators, aber man hört nichts, natürlich nicht und niemand denkt an das was die Maschinen da machen.

*Helga T. Green:* Und Sie zeichnen die Spuren, die die Besucher der Installation bei ihrem Rundgang hinterlassen ja auch auf.

*Michael Holst:* Was man heute mit Tracking machen kann ist faszinierend. Die Besucher der Installation geben ja ihre Einwilligung dazu. Sie merken das gar nicht, was da wirklich mit ihnen gemacht wird. So wie das heute überall ist: Man gibt seine Zustimmung ohne das man es wirklich merkt. Der Computer zeichnet dann alles auf. Für jeden Besucher kann man eine Karte ausdrucken, auf der der Weg, den er durch die Installation genommen hat genau aufgezeichnet ist. Man sieht, wie lange er an welcher Stelle gestanden hat und in welche Richtung er geschaut hat. Wer will kann sich so einen Ausdruck mitnehmen. Die meisten sind sehr überrascht, wenn sie den Bogen in Händen halten. Wir hatten sogar schon überlegt aus diesen Karten, diesen Bewegungs- und Aufmerksamkeitsprofilen, ein eigenes Buch zu machen.

Aber bei fast zwölftausend Besuchern wäre das ein viel zu dickes Buch geworden.

*Helga T. Green:* Hat es da Leute gegeben, die sich beschwer haben?

*Michael Holst:* Nein, erstaunlicherweise nicht. Ganz im Gegenteil, die meisten fanden das dann sehr interessant, wenn eine Mitarbeiterin ihnen erklärt hat, wie diese Linien und Kreise zustande gekommen sind, die da auf dem Bogen standen. Es hat dann in Boston sogar eine Galerie gegeben, die hat den Besuchern diese Bögen abgekauft. Also ich habe damit nichts zu tun. Ich habe nur davon erfahren, weil dieser Galerist, der ist dann später zu mir gekommen und wollte – das war noch während die Installation lief – dass ich diese Bögen signiere. Da habe ich mich aber geweigert. Wenn ein Ausstellungsbesucher etwas signiert haben will, dann ist das okay. Das mache ich gerne. Das gehört für mich dazu. Aber ein Galerist, der das dann aufkauft und im Nachhinein von mir eine Legitimation dafür haben will, das finde ich geht zu weit. Das sind ja doch ganz persönliche Daten.

## __ Resonanz

*Helga T. Green:* Wie ist die Installation aufgenommen worden? Was ist da Ihr Eindruck?

*Michael Holst:* Also wir machen da ja auch eine Umfrage unter den Besuchern. Und da war ich doch erstaunt, wie sehr sich die Leute, gerade in Amerika, auf dieses Projekt eingelassen haben und als wie befreiend sie es erlebt haben. Amerika ist ja ein Land, in dem Freiheit eine ganz wichtige Rolle spielt. Aber es ist doch so, dass es heute kaum noch wirkliche Freiheit, ich meine die Freiheit,

die im Kopf anfängt, gibt. Wir, und das denke ich ist
ein globales Phänomen, haben viel von der Freiheit, die
wir haben als Menschen, in einem ganz ursprünglichen
Sinne verloren, durch Ängste, durch falsch verstandene
Sicherheitsbedürfnisse, aber natürlich in vielen Ländern
auch ganz massiv durch Machtstrukturen, in Wirtschaft
und auch im politischen Leben, selbst in den Ländern
in denen Demokratie die Staatsform ist. Und da ist so
ein leerer Raum befreiend. Da ist er in einem ganz ursprünglichen Sinne des Wortes ein Frei-Raum. Und
den braucht jeder Mensch. Und es ist vielleicht wirklich
heute dann die wichtigste Rolle und Aufgabe der Kunst,
diesen Freiraum zu schaffen, zu ermöglichen.

*Helga T. Green:* Aber es ist ja auch etwas in ihm, diese Flusen. Zuhause würde man die einfach mit dem Staubsau-
ger wegsaugen.

*Michael Holst:* Ja, *(lacht)* das ist natürlich auch das Sauber-
keits- oder Reinemachen-Thema. Das ist ja sehr deutsch,
habe ich zumindest immer gedacht, auch in der Schweiz,
natürlich, aber auch in Amerika: Hygiene. Das ist ein
Thema, ganz aktuell. Und natürlich, der Malerlehrling,
der zum ersten Mal zum Beispiel eine Tür lackiert, der
bemüht sich natürlich darum, so wenig Flusen wie möglich im Lack zu haben. Die gehören da nicht hin. In der
Installation ist das anders. Ja, die Flusen sind auch die
kleine erlaubte, ja wichtige, Unordnung, das Anderssein,
das das Leben erst zum Leben macht. Und dann stehen
sie natürlich auch für Freiheit, für die Freiheit, die sich
nicht einsperren oder verbieten lässt. Sie sind einfach
überall, diese Flusen und so sollte das mit der Freiheit
auch sein.

*[Eine leicht gekürzte englische Fassung dieses Textes erschien am
11. April 2020 in einer Sonderbeilage des Boston Chronical.]*

# fluffs | flusen



## __ perceiving

There are statements that are bold statements. The one about the empty space, that doesn't exist, is one such bold statement, I think. It could really exist, the emptiness, the really completely empty space that one can really be afraid of, that's how I understand this dictum of the „horror vacui", which also has shown a great deal of relevance in art. But does it exist, the really empty space? Nobody can have seen it, because everywhere we look there is something, always. It could be that we produce what we see by looking, and I even think that this is probable, and if one had to take this very seriously, it would mean for my work as an artist that I wouldn't have to, shouldn't, or perhaps couldn't do it at all, because the viewer makes the art. He creates what he sees with his looking.

For a long time I found this idea very unpleasant and when I sat down and tried to create an exhibition, it hindered me, really paralysed me and I really had days I couldn't work at all, nothing happened and then – I even felt somehow a little bit like being depressive or in a deep agony – a thought came up to my mind, that maybe I'm a companion for this looking and I look too and I as well create with this looking and I can help others to see and I

129

found this a really nice thought and it drives me since then to do what I do and what is so important to me.

*[Michael Holst, September 23, 2017, Centre Max Flaubert, Paris]*

## __ it's all physics

I could have read Laplace or Descartes, probably I should have read Descartes much earlier. The inner quiet galance with which such a fluff wanders, on the fabric of the trousers for example, is easy to admire. I mean that quite honestly. There is so much life in such a small piece of matter, so much interaction with its surroundings, so much sensitiveness and sensitivity to the tensions, for example, that such a synthetic fabric exerts on a cotton lint. Of course, it's all physics and so on, but it's also simply wonderful. And it's important for me to see that.

*[Michael Holst, August 12, 2019, St. Johns Church, London]*

## __ Boston

Boston is a challenge. That was my first thought when I got the offer. Of course, I immediately said yes. But I also knew at once that it would be a real challenge. The installations in Zurich and Basel, even that in Frankfurt, which already had almost as many square meters as that in Boston, everything was still manageable somehow, the effort already enormous, but still in the range with which the team had experience. Of course we wanted to do it really well in Boston, too. The conditions there, from the facilities alone, are simply ideal. And that's why we started work at once.

It was very important to me that, as we did it for the other installations too, the interactive audio guide was individually adapted to the rooms. That is not trivial. We spent three days only measuring the acoustics of the rooms. The data model is more than three terrabytes in size. And then we had a problem with the trackers and the frequencies for transmission to the headsets. This is actually all standard technology. But the frequency bands that we had used for this in the previous projects in Europe, were not allowed to use in America. There the bands are allocated differently. No problem, we thought. The bandwidth was even a bit larger, but there was a problem with the range because of the different frequency. We practically need twice as many repeaters, which is also due to the solid construction of the Boston Conference Center. That's from 1920 and they put a lot of steel in there. As free beams, very massive and also in the concrete. And that has very interesting effects. Most of the time it swallows the electromagnetic waves. But sometimes it redirects and even amplifies them, and you have to measure every point to make sure the system works reliably.

Once we had done that, we noticed that in some rooms there was an overlay with the electric fields that we use to control the fluffs with. And it was not easy to change that. Such fluffs are not really heavy but they need a very specific electrostatic field to float. It was quite a lot of work, to find the right values that it works. And now we had to do it completely new and that in three days, a system that took us half a year to get it running reliably. That was really hard. But in the end it worked and I am really so grateful to the team for their excellent work. It was fantastic.

*[Michael Holst in January 2020 interviewed by Julian D. Richardson from New York Sculpture Magazine]*

## „The real understanding comes when you're already back home."

*by Hans Peter Markstein*

Entering the large main hall of the Bosten Conference Center, you are surprised to find yourself in a totally empty room. It is a functional building from the 1920s with large conference halls. For some time now it has been used as an exhibition center, too. Expecting to see the new installation of illustrious German artist Michael Holst, the first thing coming up in your mind is: this room is empty. And it is. A large empty rectangular room. Only after a while you do notice that there is something here after all: small, almost invisible fluffs. They lie on the floor and, as the second glance shows, still and increasingly irritated, they are found, albeit in small numbers, on the walls and on the highly mounted ventilation flaps. The fact that one notices them, after some time, has to do with the subtle way they are placed. Once you notice them, you see that they are lying everywhere, moving, whether by the perplexed viewer's walking around in this installation, in which he is looking for exhibited objects, or by a draft coming from somewhere, or perhaps – the thought comes after some time –, through electrical charge. Is it synthetic fibres floating on the floor, just above the floor, in the large free corner of the room at the back, where an imposing sculpture easily could be placed, or where there would be room for a large painting? But there is nothing of that kind. What you will find, in this room, whose emptiness is still oppressive, are light sources that are very cleverly placed in unidentifiable places. They make the fibers glow, only for a short moment, sometimes barely perceptible, then for a long time clearly visible, in a place where you just might have walked around and thought there was nothing. But that is not right. They are everywhere, these fluffs, these little fibers.

They are fragments, is the association that arises, after some time, for a reason that is not apparent. And yet the thought of the fragmentary remains present, in the mind of the viewer who walks through this installation, thinking that these small fluffs could perhaps be the remnants of a discarded garment, perhaps from a person who has lived a long time ago or whose whereabouts are unknown. What could one know about this person, about his life, his wishes and ideas, if one were to examine one of these fluffs, as precisely as is possible today, using the fine chemical methods, the microscopes and mass spectrometers? Would there be a story and how true would it be? How true could it be?

At this point there is the danger of getting lost in deep, abysmal or even boundlessly fantastic thoughts. But one should not do so. It is helpful that there is an exceptionally well-designed audio guide for this installation. At the entrance one gets handed out voluminous headphones. They have an astonishing sound quality, which may well correspond to that of reference headphones in a recording studio, and they have two small trackers, one on the right and one on the left ear cup, which transmit the position of the visitor in the room very precisely to the audio system. And so, when you walk through the installation with this technically sophisticated audio guide, the sound, speech and music will always match exactly your position in the room.

This is a completely new concept of an audio guide. Yes, actually the term audio guide is somehow a little bit misleading here. It is an individual, interactive spatial sound installation through which the visitor walks. And the headphones, which so precisely reproduce the finely mixed sound events, imperceptibly give the visitor impulses, at certain points in the installation, to slow down or accelerate his step or change his direction of gaze or walking. The transition into another room of the installation is thus organic, but is also sometimes realized as a break or surprising contrast.

You suddenly find yourself in a cold room with bright white light from the nowhere of a uniformly radiating overhigh ceiling surface. He could have called it „dust", this installation, the artist said in an interview. And in this room, one really has the impression that there is a fine dust in the air, very evenly distributed, more noticeable than visible and yet tremendously present. You want to put on a mask and wear some protective garments, you think as soon as you enter the room.

„Follow the red line" is written on a sign at the entrance of the room. And the visitor follows this instruction. The red line, neatly glued to the smoothly polished floor, seems to be the only way, the obviously only allowed, the only safe way through this danger, this danger zone with the many imponderables, which lie there in the invisible of the evenly felt fog or haze.

The atmosphere of the adjoining room is completely different, airy and light. „Gallery" is its name and the catalogue promises paintings with eloquent titles: „The Lake" should hang on wall three, „Garden House in the Snow on a Sunny Afternoon" on the wall opposite, says the catalogue. But when you are in the room, you see nothing. Again an empty room. Only if you look very closely you do notice that paintings, or more precisely large frames, must have hung on these walls for some time and left their shadow on the otherwise impeccable white of the wall. At one point of the wall, one of the workers in the exhibition, one of those involved in the construction, seems to have been careless.

It could be the trace of a dirty glove, the diagonally downward pointing strip on the left, in the lower third of the wall surface.

What makes you so attentive when you stand in this empty room? There is nothing here and yet there are so many processes, so many images in the viewer, as in no other installation. An astonishing sensitization has taken place and with this sensitively trained gaze one enters the next room. It is full of large-format canvases. At last, one thinks. There is something. Exhibits. Something you can tell people about when they ask you what you've seen during this visit, which has now already lasted over an hour. „Large formats“ is the name of the room. And they're really big these canvases. 3 meters by 4 meters the smallest. The largest, it fills the whole front wall of the room, measures 8.90 metres by 4.20 metres. It are monochrome surfaces, well stretched canvases, even the large ones, perfectly stretched without any creases or waves, and they are painted, monochrome, usually with a slightly broken white. Whether it shimmers, the colour applied to the canvases, cannot be said. There are many nuances of colour, but these are probably shadows, unevenly reflected light from the ceiling and also the viewer standing in front of the canvas takes or throws light.

Then you notice that there are fluffs on the varnish, larger and smaller fluffs in different colours. They form patterns, recede behind the white of the canvas to which they adhere and sometimes disappear completely, only to reappear unexpectedly in another place. The not-being-there, the not-more-or-not-yet of an appearance, seems to be the central theme of this installation. Normally, fluffs have no place on a painted surface. Here they fit. They relax the omnipresent white, make it seem warm, sometimes playful, but in any case cheerful. It is only through the fluffs that this room gets its light and airy cheerfulness.

The last room of this installation is called „Disappeared“, as if everything that can disappear had not already disappeared, in this exhibition. On the floor, again on the floor, there are drag marks. Heavy boxes have been carried out of here. A bounced lashing strap lies in a corner, a piece of wood broken off a wooden pallet lies next to it. In terms of volume, it is the largest exhibit in the entire installation. The workers who carried the things out here, dragged them, pushed them across the floor, wore rough shoes, they walked through mud. You can see that from the marks they left on the floor.

The light that comes evenly from the ceiling, which is a pleasant relaxation to look into and a real contrast to the traces of chaos on the floor, gives you hope. Only outside in the small inner courtyard does one become really calm again when sitting on the bench, of which one doesn't even notice that it is also part of the installation. Then you leaf through the catalogue once again, as a resonance to this emotionally so stirring walk through the empty rooms and the many millions of fluffs. And then you notice that you still have some of them on your shoes or that they have attached themselves to some of your clothes. Even days later I still find these synthetic fluffs with their intensely fluorescent colour on my clothes, also on the floor of my rooms and on the textile covers of my furniture. They attached themselves to me quite unnoticed as I walked through the seemingly empty rooms. The thought arises that this is probably the first exhibition by an artist in which it is a part of the concept of the exhibition that visitors take some of the exhibits home with them.

# _ENERGETIC

## _ Empty rooms

*by Yoko Kawakami*

It is an amazing experience that the new installation by Michael Holst conveys. Looking at blank walls, you find yourself lost in rooms completely empty. You are trying to find something, but there really is nothing. They are empty, really completely empty, these rooms. Finally at some point, you try to see a structure on the even white – the painters have done their work well, you think – but there is none, there is nothing. Right at the end, you are about to leave the room disappointed, with a smile suggesting an implied understanding, which doesn't really work, hiding the disappointment from yourself, because you don't want to admit that you didn't see anything, the ashamed look falls to the floor and you see a structure, one that interacts with your own, fleeing, shadow. That makes you turning around and just now you are realizing that you have been walking around all this time in the picture you were looking for, that you have left your marks in it, that you have helped to create it yourself, just like the many other visitors, because the picture is on the floor, is the floor and the coloured fluffs, electrostatically charged, moving back and forth on it. The floor has a special coating that generates electrostatic fields of varying intensity, fields that change and create a movement that interacts with the movement of the visitors walking through the room.

When entering the room, the fluffs have attached themselves to the soles of your shoes, and depending on how the individual zones of the floor are prepared, they are catched or released again. A constant dialogue of the steadily changing picture on the floor with the visitors walking through the picture. I wonder how many of the visitors have noticed this, and how many, as almost me, have simply walked out of the room with an elegantly hidden disappointment and perhaps only noticed at home that something has stuck to their shoes, or to their clothes. I'm happy that I'm one of those who could already notice it in the room, who had the chance to turn around again, with the view newly opened by the awareness and to take it in, this momentum that the installation creates.

A truly amazing installation, I think, and a truly extraordinary artist who, with the footsteps of his visitors, creates an image that, as a gift, is entirely his image. And then the seemingly unbearable emptiness is suddenly filled with a poetry whose immense intensity connects me with all those who have visited and will visit this installation. Currently on view in Boston until April 21.

*[This text originally was published on January, 10, 2020 in Ashi Shimbun, Tokyo. Translation: Marry Kampbell.]*

## __ Words only

*Helga T. Green:* If people want to find some information about you, on the net, for example, they will only find words. There is no picture of you as a person. You refuse to be photographed. Why?

*Michael Holst:* If you want to have this answered in one sentence, very briefly and concisely, then it is because I want my work to be the focus of attention. I don't want it to be about my person, I want it to be about what I do, as an artist.

*Helga T. Green:* You're very consistent about that. Even at exhibition openings, you always come in very different clothes, one could also say disguise. In Frankfurt you once wore a Goethe costume.

*Michael Holst:* Costume is not right. I wore what people wore in Goethe's time, as a man. Of course that has something to do with Frankfurt. If you make art in Frankfurt and you're aware of the place, not just doing something here that you could do in New York or in Boston or Sydney, then of course it has something to do with Goethe, even if you're not directly referring to him. – I've never done that. – But Goethe lived in Frankfurt, the city shaped him and if you get involved with a city, it does something to you. It did something with Goethe and it does something with me, and sometimes it's good that you put that into visual forms and that's why I wore these clothes at that exhibition. By the way, if it's well made, it's very comfortable, you can feel quite comfortable in it. And I think Goethe also felt comfortable in the clothes he wore and in the role that they, and society and his social background, his parental home, assigned to him, and which he shaped, with which he also played, even with its limitations. And he did it with an amazing success, though you may say, that he of course was quite arrogant somehow.

*Helga T. Green:* But the way you dress is also always a kind of disguise. People who have seen you at one art opening will not necessarily recognize you at the other, and certainly not if they meet you on the street. When I first met you at a press event, you wore a tailor-made suit, shirt and tie. Today you're sitting opposite me in casual jeans and a loose sweater. Are you always someone else?

*Michael Holst:* I am always the same. *(laughs)* I have no problem with that. I like to change the appearance, because it is interesting how people react to it. That's what art is about, creating a reaction in people. I'm always different in my outward appearance, because it is always a different project that I do. And these projects demand to be presented differently. As I said, it is about what I do, about the content of my works. It is not about presenting myself as a person.

*Helga T. Green:* But by practicing that strategy, you never will have the chance to develop your own brand. Can an artist today still allow himself that? There is not even an official press photo of you.

*Michael Holst:* I take the liberty, I simply do it. I am an artist. And as an artist, I take the liberty of not allowing myself to be portrayed. I can do that. And it's being accepted.

*Helga T. Green:* You once sued a journalist because he published a photo of you after an interview you gave him.

*Michael Holst:* No, that's not right. I did not sue him. I didn't have to, and the photo wasn't published. The story is always told wrong. He offered the interview to a big newspaper, also with a picture that, I didn't notice that, had been taken in the lobby of the hotel where we met. It was done by a photographer who was paid for it. But the editors called my office and asked if that was authorized and of course it wasn't and so it wasn't published. Whether the newspaper then took legal action against the journalist, I cannot say. From my side that was done.

*Helga T. Green:* And you think you can or want to go on with this, that way? You look pretty good sitting opposite me right now. You could be on a talk show sometime. I think it would be good for your art.

*Michael Holst:* No, there will be no such thing, television and all that, not even my voice in a podcast, or a radio interview. I am consistent with that. There are only the letters, if you want to know what I think about my art, how I explain it, then you have to read. The first gallery owner selling my work, right at the beginning, he wanted to „build me up" as an artist, as he said. And there are also the great role models, not only in the present, Picasso, for example. It' s well known that he promoted himself as a person, the name is more important than the work, at least that's how it developed, and I think that's what he wanted. And that's okay. And it's also an achievement if you manage it like that. But I, I don't want that. I have a different understanding of art. Art must also be able to fight back, to defend itself. I make pictures, pictures that should emerge in people's heads, when they look at them, when they visit exhibitions and installations, when they talk, discuss and think about them. I do not need a picture of myself as a person. That's what the identity card says. The identity card says nothing about me as an artist. As I said: If you want to know how I see my art, you have to read. There are just the letters. That's something really wonderful.



## __ Fluffs

*Helga T. Green:* Hans Peter Markstein, who wrote a wonderful essay about your current project „Fluffs", said at an exhibition opening with photographs of the installation, I think it was the exhibition in Frankfurt, that his thought was, that for this project you tore up the Goethe costume, and he thinks the fluffs are this costume, its remains that can't be washed away, the trace of a DNA that belongs to our culture, even if we are no longer aware of it.

*Michael Holst:* Yes, of course it's a very nice metaphor and Hans Peter Markstein writes really great texts, he's someone who empathises with what he writes about and he's someone who understands Artists and their work. And when an installation triggers such thoughts, it is simply a sign that what I'm doing there, with my exhibitions, works. In this case, however, I have to say that I am not really happy with this metaphor. He also wanted to write that in the essay, indeed he already had done that, but before publishing he wanted to talk to me about it. And that's the good thing with Hans Peter, he asks the artists when he has something he's not sure about. Other journalists or publicists don't do that. And I told him that I think that metaphor is far too specific. As an association for him, when he walks through the exhibition, I think that's completely okay. But in that kind of text, which is then also in the exhibition catalogue, I think it's simply not right. It leads the visitor in a direction that restricts his view far too much. These light floating fluffs become much too heavily charged with meaning. That's not what I want. As a text, that is simply wrong. As a fleeting thought that comes up in someone who knows my works and who has perhaps already visited some of my other installations, that's okay. But in an essay, no, that's just not right and I don't always want to be connected with the Goethe theme, just because I once wore this costume. That was over ten years ago, and that's no longer relevant.

*Helga T. Green:* Of course, when you stand in an empty room and you get all sorts of thoughts, it's hard to understand what the artist who designed this installation had in mind.

*Michael Holst:* That's right, of course, but the point is, that in this empty space, the space is there for what is in you. Today this space is almost nowhere to be found. Everything is structured, planned through, filled with content and descriptions. There are no empty spaces left in todays world. A finely structured coordinate system has been laid over our planet. Every point on it has a number, i.e. latitude and longitude, and even the cosmos has been sized, not yet as accurately as the Earth, but also astonishingly accurately. And everywhere are texts and immages and language and sounds. There's something quite extraordinary about empty space. That's how it came to me, this thought. And then I had the thought that there is something, that there is still something in this empty space. And this is what the fluffs are, these little fluffs that you hardly can see, which hardly seem to be there. But they are everywhere. You just mentioned Hans Peter Markstein and the tattered Goethe costume, so I really have to be very careful not to name such concrete images myself, but I was thinking of the string theory. It says that the world consists of these strings, one also could say filament, or even small fluffs, mathematically described fluffs in a multidimensional space.


## __ Tracking

*Helga T. Green:* You use a lot of technology in your installation. Even if it is not visible from the outside, behind what you see in the seemingly empty rooms and hear through the headphones, there is a whole arsenal of high-tech equipment. A reviewer of the Boston installation critically noted that as a visitor, one is helplessly at the mercy of this technology. Because you can't see it, you can't defend yourself against it.

*Michael Holst:* Yes, that is correct and really well observed. I didn't expect to read something like that in the American arts pages. Perhaps it's also because the installation strikes a nerve in society: you don't see the really threatening. It stands in a small box, or a metal shelf, in an adjoining room to which you have no access. If you really prick up your ears, you might hear the noise of the fans, or the hum of a transformer, but you don't hear anything, of course not, and nobody thinks about what the machines are doing.

*Helga T. Green:* And you do record the traces that the visitors of the installation leave behind when they walk around.

*Michael Holst:* What you can do with tracking today is fascinating. The visitors of the installation give their consent to it. They don't even notice what is really being done with them. Just like it is everywhere today: You give your consent without really noticing it. The computer then records everything. You can print out a map for each visitor, on which the path they have taken through the installation is exactly recorded. You can see how long they have been standing at which place and in which direction they have looked. Whoever wants to can have a printout of his tracks. Most people are very surprised when they hold the sheet in their hands. We had even thought about making an own book from these sheets, these movement and attention profiles. But with almost twelve thousand visitors, that would have been a far too big book.

*Helga T. Green:* Were there any people complaining?

*Michael Holst:* No, surprisingly not. On the contrary, most of them found it very interesting when a member of staff explained to them how these lines and circles that were on the sheet came about. There was even a gallery in Boston that bought these sheets from the visitors. Well, I have nothing to do with it. I only found out about it because the gallerist came to me later and wanted me to sign these sheets while the installation was still running. But I refused to do that. If an exhibition visitor wants something signed, then that's okay. But a gallerist who buys it and wants me to legitimize it afterwards, I think that's going too far. That's very personal data.


## __ Response


*Helga T. Green:* How was the installation received. What is your impression there?

*Michael Holst:* Well, we're doing a survey among the visitors. And I was surprised how much people, especially

in America, got involved in this project and how freeing they experienced it. America is a country where
freedom plays a very important role. But it is true that
today there is hardly any real freedom, I mean the freedom that starts in the head. I think this is a global phe-
nomenon, and we have lost much of the freedom that we
have as human beings, in a very original sense, through
fears, through a misunderstood need for security, but of
course in many countries also very massively through
structures of power, in the economy and also in politi-
cal life, even in those countries where democracy is the
form of government. And there, such an empty room is
freeing. It's an open space, a free room in a very primal
sense of the word. And everybody needs that. And it is
perhaps really the most important role and task of art
today to create this free space, to make it possible.

*Helga T. Green:* But there is actually something in it. These
fluffs. At home you would simply vacuum them away.

*Michael Holst:* Yes, *(laughs)* of course that's also the cleanliness or cleaning theme. That's very German, at least
that's what I always thought, also in Switzerland, of
course, but in America as well: hygiene. That is a topic,
very actual. And, of course, the apprentice painter who
paints a door for the first time, for example, naturally
strives to have as little fluffs in the paint as possible.
They do not belong there. It's different in the installation. Yes, the fluffs are also the small permitted, even
important disorder, the being different that makes life
real. And then of course they also stand for freedom, for
the freedom that cannot be locked up or forbidden. They

148

are simply everywhere, these fluffs, and that's the way it should be with freedom, too.

*[A lightly shortened version of this text appeared on April 11, 2020 in a special supplement of the Boston Chronical. Translation form the German original by Michael Reuters.]*

# _LANDSCHAFT

## _ „eigentlich ist alles landschaft"

*Transkript des Podiumsgesprächs, das Katrin Schubert am 11. Oktober 2021 bei der Finissage der Ausstellung „LANDSCHAFT" mit Michael Holst führte.*

*Katrin Schubert:* Lassen Sie mich mal mit einer Provokation anfangen, auch wenn Sie vielleicht sagen mögen, dass der Künstler für die Provokation zuständig ist *(lächelt)*. Ich versuche einfach einmal die Rollen zu tauschen: Landschaft, also, wenn ich die Ausstellung nicht gesehen hätte, die Faszination dieser wunderbaren Bilder, die ja manchmal fast eine magische Wirkung haben, vielleicht auch durch die Art wie sie in den Räumen präsentiert werden, also dann hätte ich wahrscheinlich gesagt: Landschaft? Was soll das? Ist das ein aktuelles Thema heute: Landschaftsphotographie?

*Michael Holst:* Ich finde das eine gute Frage und gar keine Provokation *(lacht)*. Kunstgeschichtlich ist Landschaft oder Landschaftsmalerei, Landschaftsphotographie, ja ein ganz klassisches Thema. Und klassische Themen sind wichtig, deshalb sind sie ja klassische Themen. Da habe ich gar keine Angst mich dem zu stellen. Und dann ist es einfach ein sehr vielfältiges Thema. Was um uns herum ist, ist Landschaft. Eigentlich ist alles Landschaft könnte man sagen, auch wenn das natürlich falsch ist, oder einfach eine unsinnige Definition. Aber es ist ja zum Beispiel auch immer die Frage, wann es Landschaft ist, das was ich da photographiere, und wann es zum Beispiel das Portrait eines Baumes ist, wie er da steht, in der Landschaft.

*Katrin Schubert:* Ja gut, das verstehe ich. Aber es gibt viele klassische Themen, deshalb noch einmal meine Frage: Warum Landschaft?

*Michael Holst:* Also wenn Sie eine ganz persönliche Antwort wollen, dann einfach weil ich in ihr bin und weil sie mich inspiriert. Auch weil ich mich mit ihr auseinandersetze, auseinandersetzen muss und auch will, und das mache ich eben mit der Photographie, mit der Malerei natürlich auch, aber in dieser Ausstellung, in diesem Projekt eben mit der Photographie.

*Katrin Schubert:* Es gibt auch Zeichnungen von Ihnen in der Ausstellung, auch wenn diese so auf den ersten Blick gar nicht als Zeichnungen ins Auge fallen.

*Michael Holst:* Sie meinen die Gestaltung der Wände.

*Katrin Schubert:* Ja. Das sieht ja manchmal – entschuldigen Sie, dass ich das so sage – aus wie Kratzer oder eine Verunreinigung, diese schwarzen Linien, die sich erst einmal gar nicht zuordnen lassen.

*Michael Holst:* Ja. Aber es ist ja schön, dass Sie diese Linien als Zeichnungen identifiziert haben. Und es sind in der Tat Zeichnungen. – Ich habe als Kind, schon als sehr kleines Kind, immer gerne in den Bücherschränken meiner Eltern gestöbert. – Die Neugierde ist ja etwas ganz wichtiges, und ich möchte jeden dazu ermutigen sich das beizubehalten. – Wir hatten im Wohnzimmer einen großen Schrank, so klassisch aus Eiche und im unteren Bereich des Schrankes waren vor den Fächern Türen, die ich als Kind schon gut öffnen konnte. Und da waren alles Bücher, meist größere und schwerere Bücher, Bildbände zum Beispiel. Die hatten meine Eltern da hingestellt, weil sie da auf dem Sockel des Schrankes standen und dort die Schrankböden nicht durchbiegen konnten. Schwere Bücher können ja auch recht stabile Regalbretter oder die Einlegeböden von Schränken durchbiegen. Und da gab es auch einen Bildband über steinzeitliche Höhlen, über die von den ersten Menschen bewohnten Höhlen, und da waren auch diese wunderbaren Höhlenmalereien abgebildet. Teilweise als großformatige farbige Photographien, aber auch als Zeichnungen. Ich denke das waren Zeichnungen, schwarz-weiße Strichzeichnungen, die die Archäologen zur Dokumentation angefertigt hatten. Und diese Zeichnungen sind ja sehr abstrakt. Und das hat mich als Kind schon sehr angesprochen. Und auf den Innenseiten des Buchdeckels waren auch einige Linien dieser Zeichnungen, einfach als grafisches Motiv, einige Striche, recht grob und in Rot auf dem weißen Papier, mit dem die Innenseite des Buchdeckels vorne und hinten ausgekleidet war.

Viel später, da war ich schon im Gymnasium, hat meine Mutter einmal an einem Abend in dem Buch geblättert und zu mir, als ich in den Raum kam gesagt: „Schau mal, das ist eines der Bücher in die du als Kind gemalt hast." Und ich war ganz erstaunt, denn ich war mir sicher, dass diese Zeichnungen da nicht von mir waren. Und ich habe mir die Seiten genau angeschaut und das war gedruckt. Man konnte gut das Raster des Drucks sehen. Aber meine Mutter wollte das nicht glauben, selbst als ich ihr mit einer Lupe das Raster des Druckes zeigte, hat sie es nicht geglaubt. Sie war sich ganz sicher, dass diese Linien von mir waren. Seitdem habe ich immer ab und zu einmal solche Linien gezeichnet, nicht in Bücher und nicht auf Wände, so wie das ja eigentlich bei der Höhlenmalerei ist, aber es sind daraus ganze Hefte entstanden. Ich mag ja diese kleinen Hefte, die ich immer mit mir herumtrage und in die ich immer schnell mal etwas zeichne, wenn mir etwas einfällt.

Und als ich jetzt für die Ausstellungskonzeption mir Gedanken gemacht habe, wie man die Wände gestalten könnte, die wir in die Ausstellungsräume eingebaut haben, um alle Bilder platzieren zu können, da kam mir – als das Team schon gegangen war, und ich mir noch einmal alles angeschaut habe, so um zu wissen, wie weit wir gekommen sind und was noch zu tun ist am folgenden Tag – da kam mir irgendwie der Gedanke, dass ich dachte, das ist jetzt deine Chance, hier hast du einmal so viele wunderbare Wände, auf die du diese Linien zeichnen kannst. Die Höhlenmalereien sind ja auch Landschaftsmalereien, Tiere in einer Landschaft, teilweise auch Himmel und Sterne. Einige lassen sich ja sogar einem ganz konkreten Datum, einer konkreten astronomischen Konstellation, zuordnen. Das ist schon spannend. Und jetzt, als ich so in dem Rohbau der gerade frisch gestrichenen Ausstellungswände stand, da war da dieser große Impuls in mir, da Linien einzufügen, diese Linien der Landschaften, da wo eine Linie die Geschichte einer ganzen Landschaft erzählt, so wie die Höhlenmalereien es tun, und dann habe ich wirklich angefangen diese Linien zu zeichnen, auf die frisch gestrichenen Wände. Und das war ein Akt der Genese und das hatte auch etwas Befreiendes und etwas von Heimkommen, von Ankommen nach langer Zeit oder Reise. Und erst habe ich das nur so für mich gemacht, und gedacht, morgen nimmst du einen Eimer Farbe und überstreichst das Ganze wieder und wenn die Maler kommen, am Nachmittag, um ihre Arbeit weiter zu machen – wir haben ja

154

einen sehr engen Zeitplan beim Aufbau der Ausstellung gehabt –, dann ist das alles schon wieder vergessen, abgewischt, überstrichen. Es war einfach nur so für mich. Aber dann habe ich es gelassen und so sind diese Linien in die Ausstellung gekommen.

*Katrin Schubert:* Die Präsentation ist ja durchaus eigenwillig. In jedem Fall markant. Ich habe eine ganze Reihe von Kritiken gelesen, in denen bemängelt wurde, dass in der Ausstellung jegliche Beschreibung fehlt. Es gibt keine Texte, die die Ausstellung erklären, nicht einmal eine Beschriftung der Bilder, dieses kleine Schildchen, das in jedem Museum, in jeder Ausstellung, meist unten rechts, neben dem Bild oder dem Exponat zu finden ist. Und vielleicht sagt das ja nicht viel, wenn da ein Name steht und ein Werktitel, aber ...

*Michael Holst:* ... Sie sagen das ja schon selbst, das sagt nicht viel, so ein Titel. Wobei das gar nicht stimmen muss, es gibt auch Werke, die ohne den Titel gar nicht existieren könnten. Die objet trouvé von Marcel Duchamp zum Beispiel, da entsteht das Kunstwerk erst dadurch, dass man es zum Kunstwerk macht, in dem man es als Kunstwerk benennt, ihm einen Namen gibt.

Aber zur Landschaft und warum die Bilder hier bei mir keine Titel und damit auch nicht diese kleinen Schildchen haben. Mit der Landschaft ist das ja so: Heute hat jeder Punkt auf der Erde eine Bezeichnung, zumindest eine Nummer, also die Kombination aus Breiten- und Längengrad, und die meisten Orte haben auch einen Namen, meist sogar viele und ganz unterschiedliche, die sie im Laufe der Geschichte bekommen haben, von den Menschen, die da gelebt haben oder die dahin gereist sind. Und dann gibt es ja auch für die verschiedenen Landschaften in jeder Sprache einen ganzen

Satz von Bezeichnungen: Au, Steppe, Wüste, Gebirge und so weiter, und in der Landschaftsmalerei gibt es Typen von Landschaften, die sich im Laufe der Kunstgeschichte entwickelt haben, und es gibt Künstler, die mit diesen Motiven spielen, sie variieren, karikieren oder auch einfach nur imitieren. Das ist, historisch, kunstgeschichtlich und auch einfach sprachlich – nehmen Sie nur die Ortsnamen – ein riesiges Konvolut von Bezeichnungen, von Worten, letztendlich von Buchstaben und Zahlen, mit denen wir Menschen unsere Welt über- oder durchzogen haben. Und die Digitalisierung hat das Ganze, einfach weil es technisch möglich ist, dann noch auf die Spitze getrieben. Es gibt ein sehr hoch aufgelöstes Modell von der Oberfläche der Erde. Ich kann mir praktisch von jedem Ort ein Luftbild anschauen, ziemlich detailliert, einfach in dem ich durch die Oberfläche der Internetseite eines Suchmaschinenbetreibers scrolle. Und das sagt mir dann: Es gibt nichts mehr zu entdecken, auf diesem Planeten. Es ist alles schon photographiert und kartographiert und erfasst. Als Künstler stelle ich mich dagegen. Wir brauchen einen neuen Blick. Das ist das, worum es in der Kunst geht. Und ich wollte mit diesem Landschaftsprojekt die Landschaft einfach einmal von diesem ganzen Ballast befreien, das alles ablegen, der Landschaft einfach die Möglichkeit geben, so zu sein wie sie ist, in ihrer Erscheinung in der sie auf mich trifft wenn ich in ihr stehe. Die Landschaft braucht die Namen nicht, die wir ihr gegeben haben.

*Katrin Schubert:* Jetzt kann ich aber, wenn ich ein Bild sehe, in der Ausstellung, gar nicht wissen, wo das ist, was es zeigt und ich weiß auch nicht, wann es aufgenommen worden ist. Ich weiß nicht welcher Fluss das ist, der da durch die Landschaft fließt oder wie der Berg heißt, auf dessen Kuppen ich abgeholzte Bäume sehe.

*Michael Holst:* Ja, und das soll auch so sein, weil das ist auch so, wenn ich in der Landschaft stehe, so wie ich als Künstler in der Landschaft stehe, oder wie ich denke, dass ein Künstler in der Landschaft stehen sollte, nämlich unvoreingenommen, und unvoreingenommen heißt eben auch ohne Vorwissen. Und wenn man das einmal ganz grundsätzlich sieht, dann kann man das ja gar nicht wissen, oder weiß es auch gar nicht, was dieser Berg oder der Fluss, um einmal bei den von Ihnen genannten Beispielen zu bleiben, wirklich ist, so seinem Wesen nach, seinem inneren Sein gemäß.

Es gibt einen sehr markanten Berg in den Anden – ich sage jetzt gar nicht den Namen, den wir ihm heute gegeben haben –, den haben die Ureinwohner, die in unsere Sprache Indianer heißen, was ja auch kurios ist, weil sie nie in Indien waren, sondern weil jemand, der das Land, in dem ihre Vorfahren lebten, erkunden – eigentlich in Besitz nehmen wollte – , dachte er wäre in Indien – dass diese Ureinwohner, ich sage jetzt mal wahrscheinlich die ersten Menschen, die diesem Berg begegnet sind, die ihn vielleicht erklommen haben, oder ihn immer von weitem, weil er so gut erkennbar in der Landschaft liegt, gesehen haben, dass sie ihm einen Namen gegeben haben. Ein paar Silben, Konsonanten und Vokale, in einer Kombination, die für einen heute lebenden Europäer nicht ohne Stolpern auszusprechen ist. Und da kommt natürlich die Frage: Was ist da jetzt der richtige Name? Ein Name funktioniert ja nur, wenn ich mit ihm etwas verbinde. Und wenn ich unvoreingenommen bin, wirklich unvoreingenommen, dann haben die Dinge keinen Namen. Ich weiß nichts über sie. Sie sind einfach da. Und das Schöne an der Photographie ist, dass man – das versuche ich zumindest – mit der Kamera so einen unvoreingenommenen Eindruck einfangen kann. Einen Blick von so vielen möglichen Blicken, aber eben einfach einen Blick auf ein Ding, ein Etwas, in diesem Fall eben eine Landschaft. Und deshalb stehen da keine Titel, neben oder unter den Bildern, deshalb steht da nichts, weil alles was das Bild – dieser eine Eindruck – sagt, eben in dem Bild ist. Vollständig. Da braucht es keinen Titel mehr.

*Katrin Schubert:* Ich bin in der letzten Woche einmal durch die Ausstellung gegangen und habe dabei auch die Besucherinnen und Besucher beobachtet, ihnen zugehört. Und da ist mir aufgefallen, dass, wenn sie über die Bilder geredet haben, sie diesen Bilder Namen gegeben habt: „Das Wiesenbild", oder „Der Nachtturm" zum Beispiel. Und meine Frage ist jetzt: Zeigt das nicht, dass das Konzept, mit den fehlenden Bezeichnungen so nicht funktioniert, nicht funktionieren kann?

*Michael Holst (lacht):* Nein, ganz im Gegenteil. Das ist ja etwas wunderbares, das Sie da beobachtet haben. Die Menschen sind in der Ausstellung, die sehen ein Bild, sie machen eine Erfahrung und dann sprechen sie miteinander darüber. Der Mensch ist ja ein Wesen, das auf Kommunikation angelegt ist. Niemand kann für sich alleine sein. Und dann merken sie, dass sie Bezeichnungen brauchen für diese Kommunikation, um über das zu sprechen was sie sehen, gesehen haben, ihre Erfahrung, ihren Sinneseindruck. Und dann machen sie sich diese Bezeichnungen, die ja nicht da sind, ganz spontan selbst, so wie der Bildeindruck es bei ihnen erzeugt. Und ich finde es ja klasse, dass Sie diese Beobachtung gemacht haben, auch an einem ganz normalen Ausstellungstag und nicht nur bei der Eröffnung, wo alles ganz voll war und die Leute ja auch gekommen sind um miteinander zu sprechen. Und das Beispiel, das Sie gebracht haben, „Nachtturm" das ist ja ein klasse Bildtitel, das ist einfach wunderbar, was da bei den Besuchern entsteht. Und das funktioniert, ich denke eigentlich bei jedem der durch die Ausstellung geht. Die Besucher suchen, machen sich ihre eigenen Bezeichnungen, oder wie immer man das sagen will. Wenn sie jetzt einen Atlas herausholen würden um anhand der Topographie, die das Bild zeigt, auf eine bestimmte Stelle auf ihrer Karte, einen Ort zu verweisen, und dann sagten: „Ach ja, das ist der Allalingletscher, und wahrscheinlich ein Bild aus den 1970er Jahren, weil er da noch ganz mit Schnee bedeckt ist und eigentlich sieht es schöner aus, wenn man ihn von einem etwas nördlicherem Punkt aus photographiert", ja dann wäre da etwas schiefgegangen in der Ausstellung, weil dann nicht mehr der Eindruck, so wie er ist wirkt, das Bild nicht mehr Abbild ist, sondern Zeichen für etwas das man dem Zeichen zuordnet. Das Bild wird zu einem Zeichen und das ist genau das was ich in dieser Ausstellung nicht will.

*Katrin Schubert:* Wie gehen Sie mit Kritik um? Die ist ja auch nicht immer positiv.

*Michael Holst:* Also da habe ich gar kein Problem mit. Ganz im Gegenteil. Also jetzt ganz konkret bei diesem Projekt zum Beispiel: Ein Kritiker, ich weiß jetzt im Moment gar nicht mehr wer das war *(lacht)*, – das ist dann auch so eine Art von mir damit umzugehen – also ganz konkret zu dieser Ausstellung hat es eine Besprechung gegeben, in der stand, dass die Landschaften in diesem Projekt, das stereotypischste seien, was er von mir bisher gesehen hätte. Also irgendwie so hat er sich ausgedrückt, und ich denke das war gar nicht negativ gemeint, auch wenn es nicht richtig ist, aber ich verstehe wie er darauf kommt, denn viele – nicht alle – der Bilder in der Ausstellung sind mit einem extremen Weitwinkel, also nicht Fisheye, aber eben doch so 35 mm, 24 mm, meist sogar wirklich die 24 mm, gemacht. Und es ist immer eine ähnliche Position des Betrachters, auch wenn ich da natürlich beim Photographieren immer an einem ganz anderen Ort, also in einer ganz anderen Landschaft, gestanden habe. Ich denke das ist einfach mein Blick auf Landschaft, so wie ihn dieses Projekt geprägt hat. Und dann finde ich ist es okay, wenn ein Kritiker das so schreibt. Meinen Galeristen ärgert das natürlich, wenn da etwas steht, was negativ verstanden werden kann. „Stereotyp" ist ja so für sich genommen nicht positiv, wenn man es über Kunst sagt. Und das ist ja heute mit den elektronischen Medien ganz empfindlich, alles. Da werden ja einzelne Sätze, so ganz isoliert weitergegeben und dann wird plötzlich etwas zu einem Problem, was gar kein Problem oder keine Kritik war. Aber für mich ist das okay. Ich versuche immer zu verstehen, wie jemand zu so einer Meinung oder Ansicht kommt und dann klärt sich das auf, meistens.

*Katrin Schubert:* Ich habe auch in einer Rezension gelesen, dass das ja alles gar nicht Landschaft sei, was Sie da zeigen.

*Michael Holst:* Nun ja, da hatte ich ja eben schon etwas zu gesagt, dass es gar nicht so einfach ist zu sagen oder festzustellen wo Landschaft anfängt und wo Landschaft aufhört, oder was Landschaft ist. Und natürlich photographiere ich den Baum, der da in der Landschaft steht und den Wald. Und ich denke auch die Siedlung, die Stadt oder das Dorf, die da in der Landschaft liegen, sind Teil der Landschaft. Wobei das ja schon ein Gegensatz

160

ist, Stadt und Land. – Und das ist dann ja auch immer noch eine Setzung: Landschaft gleich Land. – Und wenn ich, so wie am Anfang unseres Gespräches, sage, dass alles Landschaft ist, dann macht das definitorisch natürlich keinen Sinn, aber künstlerisch schon. Das ist das Schöne an der Kunst, dass sie auch widersprüchliche Sachen machen kann. Wenn ich mir eine Stadt anschaue, dann kann ich auf sie auch schauen als Landschaft; als gestaltete, als umgestaltete Landschaft, vielleicht auch als vereinnahmte, als besetzte, ja vielleicht auch als zerstörte Landschaft. Das kommt eben auf den Blick an. Und ich habe unterschiedliche Blicke, wenn ich photographiere. Das Wichtige als Künstler ist nur, sich dieses Blicks bewusst zu sein und ihn anderen bewusst zu machen.

*Katrin Schubert:* Ist das dann das, was die Photographien eines Künstlers unterscheiden von den Photos, die ich so als Laie mit der Kamera meines Mobiltelefons mache?

*Michael Holst:* Oh, das würde ich so gar nicht sagen. Ich weiß jetzt gerade nicht mehr von wem dieser Satz ist, dass jeder Mensch ein Künstler ist, ich glaube Andy Warhol, ja ich glaube es war Warhol, der das gesagt hat, und Beuys war das mit dem Kartoffelschälen. Also ich denke wirklich, dass jeder Mensch ein Künstler ist, der Möglichkeit nach in jedem Fall, und gerade heute, wo wir so viele technische Möglichkeiten haben, Bilder zu machen und zu be- und verarbeiten, da können auch immer mehr Menschen Fähigkeiten entwickeln, den Künstler, der sie sind, auch wirksam werden zu lassen. Und ich finde das einfach, ich sage das jetzt einmal so, wirklich dumm, wenn gesagt wird, dass das Handy die Kamera verdrängt und dass es jetzt unzählige schlechte Bilder gibt, so viele schlechte Bilder wie nie zuvor und dass niemand mehr richtig photographieren kann. Nein, das ist nicht richtig.

Ich kann mir schon für wirklich nicht viel Geld eine wirklich gute professionelle Kamera kaufen, und auch die Kameras in den Mobiltelefonen werden technisch immer besser. Das ist faszinierend. Und natürlich gibt es unzählige schlechte Bilder, fantasielos, technisch fürchterlich und ohne jede Inspiration, aber es gibt eben auch unzählige faszinierend gute Bilder, voller neuer Ideen, Blicke, Perspektiven, man muss sie nur sehen, in dem großen Bilderstrom, den wir erzeugen. Und genau das ist die Kunst. Und wenn dann jemand aus meiner Ausstellung geht, sein Mobiltelefon herausnimmt und genau das photographiert, was er da gerade sieht, dann macht er das vielleicht ein kleines bisschen anders als er das sonst gemacht hätte, vor dem Ausstellungsbesuch, und vielleicht sucht er am Abend, wenn er einem Freund eines der Bilder schicken will – das ist ja auch das faszinierende, dass wir diese Bilder an jeden Ort der Welt schicken können – dann sucht er vielleicht ein Bild aus, das anders ist als die Bilder die er sonst verschickt und das Bild hat, durch den veränderten Blick, eine Qualität bekommen die es sonst nicht hatte, und da ist der Künstler wirksam geworden.

Und mein Wunsch ist, dass die Menschen sich das erhalten, dass sie es pflegen, diese vielen kleinen Veränderungen des Blicks und ihre Fähigkeit sich dessen bewusst zu werden, und es sichtbar werden zu lassen, zum Beispiel auch in einem Handy Photo und vielleicht kaufe ich mir dann einmal eine Kompaktkamera oder eine spiegellose Systemkamera mit einem guten Objektiv. Und dann entwickle ich da meine Fähigkeiten. Oder ich nehme einen Stift, das ist ja auch eine Reaktion, und

162

fange an die Linien, die ich auf dem Bild, die ich in meiner Umgebung, sehe, zu zeichnen und dann beginnt Kunst und dazu möchte ich alle Besucherinnen und Besucher der Ausstellung einladen. Ich habe nicht den Anspruch der bessere Künstler zu sein. Kunst ist nicht elitär, jeder Mensch kann Kunst machen und ich finde jeder Mensch sollte das auch machen.

*Katrin Schubert:* Welche Rolle spielt Zeit für Sie wenn Sie Landschaft photographieren?

*Michael Holst:* Landschaft ist Zeit. Das ist meine Erfahrung. Landschaft verändert sich kontinuierlich, immer, und diese Veränderung findet in ganz unterschiedlichen Geschwindigkeiten statt. Gerade mit Licht und auch Wind sind es enorme Geschwindigkeiten, die Landschaft erlebt. Es gibt so eine Vorstellung, dass Landschaft etwas Statisches sei, lange Belichtungszeiten und so weiter. Aber für mich stimmt das nicht. Es kann sein, dass ich ein Motiv sehe, und in der kurzen Zeit, die ich brauche um meine Kamera hervorzuholen – ich bin da eigentlich recht schnell –, hat sich schon alles verändert.

Es gibt aber auch die langsamen Veränderungen. Manchmal komme ich an eine Stelle, an der ich vor einem, vor zwei oder auch vor drei Jahren eine Aufnahme gemacht habe. Es gibt so bestimmte Bilder, die begleiten mich. Sie sind in mir, auch wenn ich an ganz anderen Orten bin. Und es kommt dann vor, dass ich einfach Sehnsucht nach diesem Ort habe, so wie er in meiner Erinnerung ist. Ich will noch einmal dahin, es noch einmal sehen, die Luft spüren, vielleicht den charakteristischen Geruch und den Blick. Und dann ist – ich möchte fast sagen: natürlich – alles anders oder vieles. Es können kleine Veränderungen sein, Jahreszeiten, Witterung, Tageszeit, aber es können auch radikale Veränderungen sein. Der Wald ist weg. Da ist nur noch ein gerodeter Hang, der von monströs groben Reifen zerfurchte Boden. Im Moment ist das sehr oft der Fall, gerade da wo Fichte stand. Und dann muss man sich erst einmal einsehen, durchatmen. Da ist dann Trauer, aber auch, bei mir funktioniert das so wenn ich die Kamera in der Hand habe, das ist für mich eine Hilfe, weil es ein Werkzeug ist, das mir sagt: mach etwas mit mir, nutze mich, du hast einen Job. Und dann mache ich etwas daraus. So sind gerade in den letzten zwei Jahren viele Landschaftsbilder entstanden. Auch viele traurige. Das will ich gar nicht bestreiten. Und da sind wir wieder bei der Zeit, das war ja Ihre Frage. Eine der wesentlichen Eigenschaften der Zeit ist, dass sie vergeht. Wenn sie nicht verginge, wäre es keine Zeit. Ohne Vergehen gibt es keine Zeit. Und wenn ich mit der Kamera aus der Zeit Bilder herausnehme, die ja auch wieder in der Zeit sind, sie altern ja auch, die digitalen Bilder sehr viel langsamer als die analogen, so in der Regel. Aber digitale Bilder können auch ganz radikal altern, bei einem Datenverlust altern sie von einem Moment auf den anderen so extrem, dass sie nicht mehr sind. Das ist ja auch alles sehr fragil, unsere digitale elektrische Art aufzuzeichnen.

In den Museen gibt es ja diesen Diskurs von Kunsthistorikern und vor allem von Konservatoren und Restauratoren, wie weit man in den Alterungsprozess eines Kunstwerks eingreifen soll, darf. Wie ist das mit der Patina zum Beispiel, ist so eine Frage. Meine Photographien sind alle digital. Sie werden keine Patina bekommen. Vielleicht kann man einige Dateien irgendwann nicht mehr vollständig lesen und einige Pixel sind weiß oder magenta oder einige Stellen des Bildes haben schwarze Streifen. Aber am wahrscheinlichsten ist es, dass sie dann irgendwann einfach gar nicht mehr lesbar sein werden, weil der Datenträger kaputt ist oder es die Software nicht mehr gibt, mit der man die Bilder auf einem Monitor oder einem Belichter sichtbar machen kann. Das ausbelichtete Bild, also zum Beispiel der Satz von ausbelichteten Bildern, den ich jetzt für die Ausstellung erstellt habe und die Exemplare, die in die Galerie kommen, für den Verkauf, die gibt es jetzt und die altern, so wie es die chemischen Prozesse der Materialien, aus denen sie bestehen bewirken. Man wählt dafür ja möglichst Materialien aus, die sehr alterungsbeständig, lichtbeständig und so weiter sind, und das ist ja schon ganz erstaunlich, welche Qualität heute zum Beispiel ein professionelles Photopapier haben kann, oder auch ein Ink-Print. Aber auch das altert natürlich und ich finde das soll es auch. Ja, man kann und soll sich gegen die Veränderungen, gerade gegen die, die nicht gut sind, wehren; aber man muss auch Veränderung akzeptieren. Das ist wirklich ein schwieriges Gleichgewicht. Und, dieses Gleichgewicht zwischen sich Aufbäumen, Aufbegehren, Widersprechen und dem einfachen Akzeptieren, das versuche ich in meinen Bildern zu finden. Sie sind für mich so etwas wie ein Maß, eine Linie, die mir da Halt gibt in diesem Schwingen der Zeit.

*Katrin Schubert:* Was mich überrascht hat ist die, ich sage einmal, sehr unkonventionelle Hängung. Ich meine besonders die, ich will es einmal so sagen, ungleichmäßige Verteilung der Bilder auf die Ausstellungsfläche. In dem großen Saal, dem größten Raum der Ausstellungsfläche, da hängt nur ein einziges Bild. Mit seinen – ich habe das extra noch einmal nachgeschaut – vier Meter dreißig mal knapp zwei Meter neunzig ist es zwar wirklich groß. Aber den Saal füllt es nicht. Da wäre noch viel Platz für weitere Bilder. Andere Räume sind sehr eng behängt, da sind Stellwände eingebaut, fast ein Labyrinth. In dem zweiten Saal zum Beispiel, der viel kleiner ist, da hängen zehn Bilder, auch große Formate. Warum ist das so?

*Michael Holst:* Ich denke, das hat etwas mit Rhythmus zu tun. Ich habe, als wir das Konzept für die Hängung entwickelt haben, wirklich mit dem Saal 1 angefangen. Und die Bilder sind ja extra für die Ausstellung ausbelichtet. Es stand also auch noch gar nicht die genaue Größe fest, zumindest nicht bei allen Bildern. Wir haben uns erst einmal die Grundrisse angeschaut, und im Team war da auch die Vorstellung, einfach eine möglichst gleichmäßige Verteilung hinzubekommen, so dass jedes Bild seinen Platz hat, den es braucht um betrachtet zu werden. Und das wäre auch ein gutes Konzept gewesen, einfach auch um die Geschichte, die diese Bilder in ihrer Abfolge, in ihrem Aufeinanderbezogensein, erzählen, erfahrbar zu machen.

Doch als ich zum ersten Mal in den Räumen war – es war tatsächlich der große Saal der erste Raum in dem ich war –, da wusste ich, ich will ein wirklich großes Bild hier haben in diesem riesigen Raum und nur eines und es soll nicht groß wirken. Jeder soll sich fragen, wo die anderen Bilder sind, und von daher finde ich Ihre Frage gut. Das zeigt mir, dass das Konzept funktioniert hat. – Das Bild ist groß, und so hat es auf Sie ja auch gewirkt, aber der Raum ist größer. Und das ist doch eine Aussage. Es ist Landschaft, was da im Mittelpunkt der Ausstellung steht. Und dieses wirklich große Landschaftsbild hängt in einem Raum, der größer ist als das Bild, der einen voluminöseren, ich will nicht sagen gewaltigeren, Eindruck macht als die Landschaft. Das ist unser Verhältnis zur Landschaft, heute. Wir haben sie vereinnahmt, in den Raum unseres ergreifenden Verstehens gestellt. Aber genau damit haben wir eigentlich dann nichts verstanden.

Und jetzt zu den anderen Räumen. Die sind ja alle sehr unterschiedlich gestaltet. Ich habe auch von einer Besucherin die Rückmeldung bekommen, dass sie meinte, sie sei in dieser einen Ausstellung auf ganz unterschiedlichen Ausstellungen gewesen. Einfach weil jeder Raum so individuell gestaltet ist, beziehungsweise, die Bilder immer nach ganz anderen Konzepten gehängt sind. Und das ist die Sache mit dem Rhythmus. Eine Ausstellung muss pulsieren. Und ich habe ja hier keinen vorgeschriebenen oder empfohlenen Rundgang, wie es das bei vielen meiner anderen Ausstellungen gibt. Wir haben das diesmal bewusst frei gestaltet und die Architektur gibt das ja auch her. Ich kann von jedem Saal in jeden anderen gelangen, fast immer direkt, manchmal mit einem kleinen Umweg durch einen Flur, eine Galerie oder einen Treppenaufgang, wo dann auch ein paar Bilder hängen, die mich überleiten oder vielleicht auch ablenken. Und wenn ich dann zum Beispiel, eine Möglichkeit, von dem großen Saal 1 in den Saal 4 komme – der ja wesentlich kleiner ist –, da hängen dann über 50 Bilder. Ich hätte beinahe gesagt kleine Bilder, dabei ist das gar nicht richtig, sie sind auch meist mindestens so 60 mal 60 Zentimeter, die Panoramen dann auch schon mal so ein Meter dreißig oder breiter. Und sie hängen so, dass man immer genug Platz hat sie richtig zu betrachten. Durch die eingebauten Wände sind da ganz viele intime Räume entstanden, Schau-Räume, mit individuellem Licht, so wie es jedes Bild braucht. Man kann da, ohne große Wege, das war die Idee, sehr schnell sehr viel sehen.

Es gibt ja diese Räume mit Normlicht, die man nutzt um digitale Bilder zu entwickeln oder z.B. für die Druckvorstufe auszufiltern. Wir haben praktisch um jedes Bild so einen Raum herumgebaut, den Raum den eine Person braucht, um dieses Bild optimal betrachten zu können und das in einer entspannten, inspirierenden Atmosphäre. Es gibt ja auch immer bequeme Sitzgelegenheiten, die alle individuell gestaltet sind. Da haben wir viel für getan. Das war wirklich eine Herausforderung, und das Team hat das einfach klasse umgesetzt. Sie können das ja einmal ausprobieren: Gehen Sie einfach ganz langsam durch die Räume die für die Ausstellung in diesen Saal eingebaut, ich möchte fast sagen hineingewachsen, sind, die sind ja organisch verteilt, und dann werden Sie merken, dass Sie den Rhythmus der Hängung spüren können. Und wenn Sie aus dem großen Saal 1 kommen, dem wir seine Volumiosität gelassen haben, dann merken Sie hier, in der Verdichtung, dass Sie als Besucherin die Kapazität haben, diese Dichte aufzunehmen. Sie sehen viel und Sie sehen intensiv und variantenreich und es ist keine Überforderung. Im Gegenteil, es gibt eine Ruhe.

*Katrin Schubert:* Wo wir schon von den Bildern in Saal 4 gesprochen haben. Vielleicht sagen Sie noch etwas zu den Dualen. Ich denke, die erklären sich nicht so aus sich heraus.

*Michael Holst:* Oh, vielleicht tun sie das doch, sie sollten es, zumindest die Bilder. Mit der Bezeichnung, Duale, da ist das schon etwas anders. Das verstehe ich. Das ist aber auch okay. Duale ist ein Begriff oder ein Wort, das ich von Paul Julius Kleiber übernommen habe. Und das hat erst einmal mit Landschaft gar nichts zu tun und auch nicht mit Photographie. Ich habe mich ja, gerade als

Zeichner, der ich ja auch bin, eine Zeit lang sehr intensiv mit Paul Julius Kleiber beschäftigt. Er hat, da gibt es einen wunderbaren sprachwissenschaftlichen Aufsatz von Michale Antenberg, eine sehr eigene Begrifflichkeit für seine Zeichnungen entwickelt. Wenn er auf einen Bogen sich ineinander verknäulende Liniengewirre zeichnet und er dann zwei dieser Gebilde nebeneinander entstehen lässt, dann nennt er das Dual. Das sind ja Zeichnungen, auf einem Bogen Papier oder Karton. Wenn man daraus ein klassisches Gemälde machen würde, in einem Format von eins-zwanzig mal eins-zwanzig, zum Beispiel, so ein typisches Maß für eine Ausstellung, und dann zwei dieser quadratischen Leinwände nebeneinander hängen würde, dann würde man das einfach Dyptichon nennen. Und bei mir war das jetzt so, dass ich, als ich dieses Konzept von den aufeinander bezogenen Landschaftsteilen, oder auch sich von einander oder auseinander herleitenden Landschaftsteilen entwickelt habe, ich an Kleibers Duale denken musste und da habe ich mir einfach erlaubt seinen Begriff da zu nehmen.

*Katrin Schubert:* Die meisten Duale sind ja quadratisch oder annähernd quadratisch, und meistens gibt es da eine Wiederholung. Das fällt so ganz auf den ersten Blick gar nicht immer auf, aber meist sind da Teile, die auf dem einen Bild zu sehen sind auch im anderen zu finden.

*Michael Holst:* Ich muss da jetzt etwas vorsichtig sein, um keinen Missverständnissen Vorschub zu leisten. Also vielleicht sicherheitshalber vorweg: Die Duale sind keine Stereobilder und sie sollen es auch nicht sein. Aber eine spezielle Art der Stereophotographie war für mich eine Inspiration für diese Art der Bildpräsentation. Die Stereophotographie ist ja schon eine sehr alte Technik. Da werden von demselben Motiv, meist gleichzeitig mit zwei Kameras, zwei Aufnahmen aus einer genau um den Abstand der Augen versetzen Position gemacht. Und es gibt diese wunderbaren Karten, auf denen dann zwei quadratische Bilder, eben diese beiden Aufnahmen, nebeneinander ausbelichtet werden und man mit einer speziellen Brille, in die diese Karte gesteckt wird, sich das dann anschauen kann. Und ich habe einmal bei einem befreundeten Photographen so eine ganze Sammlung solcher Karten gesehen, aus den Anfängen der Photographie, auf diesem alten Photopapier, das durch das Silberoxyd seine so wunderbare Färbung bekommt, das aber auch heute noch sehr stabil ist. Und seitdem finde ich so eine Präsentation von zwei quadratischen Bildern nebeneinander immer sehr interessant, auch wenn es keine Stereophotographien sind.

Jetzt ist das Quadrat aber eigentlich wirklich nicht das klassische Format für Landschaftsdarstellungen. Landschaft ist länglich. Sie können ein Stadtpanorama auf ein Lineal drucken und an Touristen als Souvenir verkaufen. Je länger je besser. Wenn ich jetzt zwei Quadrate nebeneinander hänge, dann hole ich mir damit gewissermaßen die Breite zurück. Vielleicht sind es auch einfach zwei quadratische Fenster, die da nebeneinander sind und ich schaue durch sie in oder auf die Landschaft. Bei einigen der Duale ist das auch wirklich so. Es sind einfach zwei quadratische Ausschnitte eines Landschaftsbildes. Da gibt es dann auch keine Wiederholung.

Bei vielen der Duale habe ich das aber auch so gemacht, dass ich einfach ein Quadrat auf den linken Teil eines Bildes gelegt habe und dann fehlt da rechts natürlich etwas von der Landschaft, und für den zweiten Dual habe ich dann einfach das Quadrat links auf das Bild gelegt und rechts fehlt etwas, aber auf beiden Ausschnitten

findet sich gemeinsam etwas vom mittleren Teil des
Bildes. Und das hat, eben mit der von Ihnen bemerkten
Wiederholung, etwas Entspannendes, Beruhigendes. Irgendwie werden die Bilder auch formaler, wenn sie so
nebeneinander hängen. Es gibt dann auch, das ist insbesondere für die Galerie wichtig, immer einen Maßstab
mit dem Abstand, in dem die beiden Bilder zueinander
hängen sollen. Und, das ist auch so eine Sache, die für
meinen Galeristen zunächst schwierig war: man kann
immer nur beide Duale zusammen kaufen. Mir war
das wichtig. Man kann diese Bilder nicht auseinander-
reißen. Mein Galerist meinte, das sei ja etwas, was man
dem Kunden zusätzlich erklären müsste. Aber ich finde
das okay und ich habe auch den Eindruck, dass die Interessenten das verstehen.

*Katrin Schubert:* Heute ist es ja praktisch in jedem Museum,
in jeder Ausstellung von Kunst so, dass dort das Photographieren verboten ist. Hier bei Ihnen, bei dieser Ausstellung, ist das anders. Warum?

*Michael Holst:* (lacht) Nun, das hat einen ganz einfachen
Grund: Ich photographiere selbst sehr gerne in Museen
und bei Ausstellungen, Messen und so weiter; an Orten, zu denen Menschen kommen, um sich Dinge anzuschauen. (Wieder ernst.) Also man kann da wirklich
wunderbare Photos machen, von den Menschen, die da
so aufmerksam in die Betrachtung vertieft sind, die sich
miteinander austauschen, über das was sie da sehen und
dann versteht man auch das Gezeigte noch einmal auf
eine ganz andere Weise. Aber das ist hier natürlich nicht
der eigentlich Grund *(lacht).* – Na, vielleicht doch. –
Wobei, ich könnte ja in meiner eigenen Ausstellung auch
photographieren, wenn das für die Besucher verboten
wäre. – Aber ernsthaft: Heute hat ja praktisch jeder sein

Handy dabei und das hat in der Regeln eine klasse Kamera, wir haben ja schon darüber gesprochen. Und der ganz natürliche Reflex ist doch, dass man, wenn man etwas Schönes sieht, etwas das einem gefällt, dieses Gerät , das man ja sowieso fast die ganze Zeit des Tages in der Hand, zumindest immer griffbereit, hat, hervorholt, und von dem was man da gerade schön, interessant, wichtig, wie auch immer, findet ein Photo macht. Und warum soll ich den Leuten das verbieten? Ganz im Gegenteil. Ich will sie ja dazu ermutigen, Bilder zu machen, ihren Blick für gute, für spannende, interessante, inspirierte Bilder zu schärfen, und da ist es doch wunderbar, wenn ich da schon in der Ausstellung mit anfange.

*Katrin Schubert:* Und wie sieht das mit den Urheberrechten aus? Als Künstler können Sie doch nicht einfach darauf verzichten? Das ist doch ein großes Thema, auch wirtschaftlich und rechtlich.

*Michael Holst:* Nun das mache ich ja auch nicht. Dass man in der Ausstellung photographieren darf, heißt ja nicht, dass man meine Bilder reproduzieren darf. Ja, es ist so, dass die Kameras, auch die kleinen und handlichen und auch die in den Mobiltelefonen, immer besser werden. Aber wenn ich eine wirkliche Reproduktion von einem Bild, das da in der Ausstellung hängt, machen will, dann muss ich doch alles richtig ausleuchten, da darf niemand vorbeigehen, oder einen Schatten drauf werfen. Es gibt immer Reflexionen die stören. Damit ich keine Paralaxenverzerrung habe muss ich den richtigen Winkel haben. Bei den großen Bildern müsste ich eine Leiter nehmen, um die richtige Position zu haben und selbst dann: das von mir als Künstler ausbelichtete Original ist dann doch ganz anders als das was ich bekomme, wenn ich von meinem Handy-Photo einen Abzug mache. Und ich denke, die Leute, die sich für Kunst interessieren, die wissen das auch.

Und wer einen Eindruck von der Ausstellung mit nach Hause nehmen will, wer vielleicht gerade eine interessante Szene mit den Besuchern der Ausstellung, ihrer Art wie sie im Raum stehen, wie sie das Licht reflektieren und ein Bild betrachten einfängt, der soll das tun. Das ist ja dann auch sein Kunstwerk und ich finde es einfach wunderbar und auch Sinn einer Ausstellung, dass dann eben auch mein – ja urheberrechtlich geschütztes – Bild auf diesem Bild zu sehen ist. Und wenn dieses, mein, Bild dazu geführt hat, dass die Szene im Raum der Ausstellung so passiert ist, ja, das ist natürlich das, was mein Anteil an der Kunst ist. Aber ohne die Besucher ist eine Ausstellung nichts und ohne die Menschen, die sich meine Bilder anschauen sind meine Bilder nicht das was sie sein sollen und deshalb freue ich mich, wenn Menschen das photographieren, sie das Bild, das da bei ihnen entstanden ist, im Kopf, zunächst, mit dem Gerät, dem Mobiltelefon oder der Kompaktkamera, mit dem was sie gerade dabei haben, mit nach Hause nehmen.

Und dann ist da ja immer noch die Sache mit der Veröffentlichung. Auch da habe ich nichts dagegen, und das steht auch am Eingang der Ausstellung und an der Garderobe und es gibt Zettel, wo das Ganze auch noch einmal erklärt ist, juristisch exakt und ich denke auch verständlich. Wenn ich in der Ausstellung photographiere, Bilder so für mich mache, dann ist das überhaupt kein Problem, und gerne auch mal einen Abzug oder einen Ausdruck, den ich mir über den Schreibtisch hänge. Und wenn ich eines der Bilder an einen Freund schicke, per E-Mail oder über einen Messenger, auch in die ganze Gruppe, Freunde, Familie, Arbeitskollegen und so weiter, dann ist das alles okay. Auch ein privater Post in den sozialen Medien, das ist okay. Das ist ja auch gut für uns, für die Ausstellung. Ich will doch keinem verbieten über das was er erlebt hat, was ihn begeistert, zu reden, sich mitzuteilen. Und heute sind das eben viele Kanäle und da gehören Photos ganz selbstverständlich dazu. Das ist doch klasse.

Es gibt da dann natürlich noch das Problem mit den Persönlichkeitsrechten der Abgebildeten. Da gibt es ja die Regel, dass wenn die einzelne Person nicht mehr als Individuum erkennbar ist, sondern es eine Gruppe von Menschen ist, die da abgebildet ist – man nimmt da immer an, dass das so ab sieben Personen ist – dann ist das mit den Persönlichkeitsrechten kein Problem mehr. Wenn ich aber eine einzelne Person abbilde, dann geht das natürlich nicht ohne deren Einverständnis. Deshalb weisen wir die Besucherinnen und Besucher der Ausstellung darauf hin, dass in der Ausstellung photographiert werden darf, und dass die Möglichkeit besteht, dass sie auf den dabei entstehenden Bildern abgebildet werden. Gleichzeitig bitten wir die Besucherinnen und Besucher, möglichst nicht einzelne Personen zu photographieren, außer natürlich, es sind Bekannte oder Freunde die das wollen. Es gibt übrigens ein Bild, das haben mir die Mitglieder des Teams erzählt, die immer in der Ausstellung sind, vor dem besonders viele Besucher gerne ein Selfie machen. Ich sage jetzt aber nicht welches Bild das ist.

*Katrin Schubert:* Und wie ist das mit einer kommerziellen Verwendung?

*Michael Holst:* Das geht natürlich nicht. Wenn jemand das machen will, dann müssen wir über eine Lizenz sprechen, und die ist dann eben auch mit Kosten verbunden. Für diese Ausstellung hatten wir da zwei Anfragen

174

und das war denen zu teuer, was ich gar nicht verstehen kann, denn so hoch war der Preis gar nicht, aber es muss ja im gerechten Verhältnis zu dem erwarteten Gewinn stehen. Wer mit meiner Arbeit Geld verdient, der soll von dem was er da mit dem was ich gemacht habe verdient, auch einen Anteil an mich geben. Ich arbeite ja nicht umsonst. Das kann ich ja gar nicht. Als Künstler bin ich ja auch Unternehmer und ich finde, es gehört auch zur Kunst, dass man die Kunst so macht, dass man mit ihr, von ihr, auch leben kann. Man bringt ja seine Lebenszeit, seine Ideen, seine Kraft und Kreativität ein. Also, das ist für mich eine Frage der Gerechtigkeit. Und ich bin auch der Meinung, dass man da gar nichts mit Verboten regeln muss. Wenn zum Beispiel Reproduktionen meiner Bilder auftauchen würden, die aus in der Ausstellung gemachten Photographien hergestellt worden sind, dann fällt das ja auf, und diese Bilder lassen sich auch nicht verkaufen, und da würde dann mein Galerist auch gegen vorgehen. Also da habe ich gar keine Sorge.

*Katrin Schubert:* Zum Schluss vielleicht noch einmal eine kritische Frage. Ich habe von einigen Ausstellungsbesuchern gehört, dass sie da etwas vermissen, in der Ausstellung. Oder eben auch etwas anderes noch, zusätzlich, erwartet hätten. Ich meine, die Besucherinnen und Besucher waren ja alle sehr begeistert, das ist schon richtig, das hat man auch in der Ausstellung gemerkt. Die Atmosphäre war wirklich an allen Tagen großartig und vielfach elektrisierend, so hat ein Besucher das gesagt, als ich mit ihm über seine Erfahrung sprach. Aber gerade deshalb wurde doch auch etwas vermisst. Es kam von einigen Besuchern auch die Frage, ob das vielleicht sogar beabsichtigt war und gerade deshalb die Ausstellung, auch in der Spannung zu ihrem Titel, Landschaft, da einen Bruch erzeugt hat, vielleicht eben auch beabsichtigt: Es gibt keine Wüsten und keine Gletscher, das Exotische fehlt. Afrika, Amerika, Australien, Asien. Da fehlen ganze Kontinente. Warum?

*Michael Holst:* Ja, das ist eine sehr wichtige Frage. Und das bin auch ich oft gefragt worden. Es war nicht die häufigste Frage, aber eine, die ich oft gestellt bekommen habe. Und ja, wenn ich den Titel „Landschaft" höre, als Titel für eine Ausstellung von Photographien, dann kommt da natürlich die Erwartung von Exotischem, von Wüsten, zum Beispiel, großartigen Dünenpanoramen der Sahara, wo die Sonne den Sand zum Glühen bringt und wo ich beim Betrachten des Bildes meine, dieses Glühen noch spüren zu können. Oder ich denke an ein Bild, in dem, an einem, sagen wir mal, schon tiefdunklen Himmel über einer von der Dämmerung bereits fast vollständig verschluckten Steppe, ein einzelner Stern dem Betrachter in die Augen glitzert. Oder an die faszinierenden Felsenformationen des Grand Canyon, in die ich mit der Kamera hineinstürze und diesen Sturz so in einem großformatigen Bild inszeniere, dass der Betrachter noch den Druck in der Magengegend spürt, den ich als Photograph gehabt haben muss, als ich diese Bilder gemacht habe.

Ja, ich denke, da gibt es tausende von Bildern, die da als Erwartung entstehen, wenn die Worte „Landschaft" und „Photographie" zusammen kommen. Aber das hier jetzt ist ja Kunst, was ich da mache, nicht Reiseberichterstattung. Und das Reisen, wie wir es heute betreiben, ich bin da durchaus auch sehr selbstkritisch, hat ja etwas Koloniales. Das Exotische wird ja nur dadurch zum Exotischen, weil wir es als solches ansehen, als solches aufsuchen, mit unserer Reise. Also, im besten Fall noch als Bildungsreise, im schlimmsten Fall als Eroberung. Und unsere Reisen haben ja auch etwas Eroberndes. Und für diese Ausstellung wollte ich – von daher ist das eine sehr wichtige, eine sehr gute Frage, zum Abschluss –, für diese Ausstellung wollte ich, dass, – ich war mir ja der Erwartung bewusst, die der Titel erzeugt – da wollte ich, dass man wenn man mit diesem - ich sage das jetzt einmal so – Sensations-Blick in die Ausstellung geht, dass man dann auf etwas trifft, dass man so sehen kann, beziehungsweise, das ich so sehe, in meinem Alltag, in der Welt in der ich mich bewege.

Und dann muss ich jetzt natürlich etwas zu meinem Reisen sagen. Ich denke, das ist unvermeidlich, wenn man eine Ausstellung mit dem Titel „Landschaft" macht: Ich bin sehr lange sehr viel gereist, so wie wir privilegierten Europäer und Nordamerikaner z. B. das tun. Und das ist natürlich dann auch viel das Flugzeug und ich habe ja auch viele Projekte in Asien gemacht, einiges auch in Afrika, vor allem Südafrika und dann auch Amerika. Und wenn man sich dann einmal die Kilometer anschaut, die man da zurücklegt, und die Zeit, die man da braucht, dann ist das schon ganz klar, dass man da ungeheure Ressourcen für verbraucht.

Einmal die Materialien, das ist einfach ungeheuerlich, wenn man das mal, also den Kraftaufwand zum Beispiel, in die Kraft umrechnet, die Menschen so mit ihren Muskeln erzeugen können. Also ich weiß gar nicht wie viele Menschen da zum Beispiel eine Stunde mit einer Kurbel einen Dynamo drehen müssten um so viel Strom zu erzeugen, dass man damit eine Stunde Auto, zum Beispiel nur mit 50 Stundenkilometer, fahren kann. Und über den Atlantik, da braucht man ein oder zwei

Wochen wenn man das mit einem Segelschiff macht, und da nutzt man ja schon die Kraft des Windes. Und wenn man das mit einem Kajak macht, also wirklich nur die Muskelkraft, dann dauert das knapp hundert Tage, also etwas mehr als drei Monate. Und da bewegt man nur ein kleines Boot und seinen Körper und wir jagen heute in acht Stunden oder sogar weniger über diese Strecke, mit einer Maschine die so 40 Tonnen wiegt.

Wenn man das mal umrechnet, wie viel Menschen dafür rudern müssten. Das ist unglaublich und da nehmen wir Menschen, also der privilegierte Teil von uns, da nehmen wir uns ein wirklich unglaublich großes Stück Ressource und zwar auf eine Art und Weise, wie wir das nie zurückbekommen werden. Wir zerstören. Und mir ist da einfach bewusst geworden, dass das in seinem ganz tiefen Kern etwas mit Einstellung zu tun hat, mit dem Blick, den wir auf das Leben, auf unser Leben hier auf diesem kleinen so verletzlichen Planeten werfen, zu tun hat. Und deshalb habe ich für mich beschlossen, das zu ändern. Einfach für mich, in meinem Leben. Und so ein Entschluss hat Auswirkungen eben auch auf das, was ich als Künstler mache.

Ich steige eben nicht mehr in ein Flugzeug und ich habe zum Beispiel für diese Ausstellung nur Bilder ausgewählt, die ich an Orten gemacht habe, die ich mit meiner eigenen Muskelkraft erreicht habe, also zu Fuß, ich bin ein begeisterter Wanderer, und mit dem Fahrrad, das habe ich wirklich lieben gelernt. Ja, ich habe das Atelier in Frankfurt, und das Atelier in Köln, jetzt ja schon seit einigen Jahren, und das ist einfach für mich auch eine wirklich tolle Chance, wenn jemand sagt: Hey ich will, dass Du nach Köln kommst, in der Stadt gute Arbeitsbedingungen hast und hier Kunst machst. Und dann fahre ich natürlich hin und her, zwischen den beiden Standorten. Aber ich versuche das schon so zu organisieren, dass ich Fahrten reduziere, dass ich nicht, wie früher zwei oder dreimal die Woche hin und her fahre, sondern vielleicht nur ein- oder zweimal im Monat und dann auch immer mit dem Zug und nicht mehr mit dem Flieger, was ja jetzt auch völlig unsinnig ist, wenn ich mit dem Zug in 50 Minuten aus Frankfurt in Köln bin, da bin ich im Flieger ja nicht einmal eingecheckt, also etwas übertrieben, aber manchmal kann das schon stimmen. Von daher hat das mein Leben sehr verändert und damit auch meine Kunst.

Und die Veränderung geht noch weiter. Und da kann man auch Technik nutzen, positiv. Also ich habe ja zum Beispiel viele Kunden im asiatischen Raum, Sammler, die sich für meine Bilder interessieren und einige haben sogar den Ehrgeiz, zum Beispiel von jeder Photographie, die von mir in einer Ausstellung gezeigt wird, einen Print zu haben, der noch zweistellig in der Nummerierung ist, also maximal die Nummer 99 eines Bildes. Und früher habe ich die Bilder bei mir ausbelichtet, signiert und verschickt. Jetzt haben wir eine Möglichkeit gefunden, die Bilder auch digital signieren zu können. Und das wird auch akzeptiert, von den Menschen die Kunst sammeln, und so habe ich jetzt vor Ort einen Dienstleister, der die Bilder ausdruckt und dann kann der Sammler das Bild dort abholen und über das Netzwerk, das wir da nutzen können, gibt es die Garantie, dass der Weg für die Verschickung nie mehr als 230 km ist. – Also das sind 200 Meilen, die Amerikaner rechnen ja gerne immer noch in Meilen, und deshalb die 230 km. – Und ich finde das ist doch schon mal ein kleiner Schritt und von diesen kleinen Schritten brauchen wir viele, damit es ein großer Schritt wird und ich denke, den brauchen wir und zwar sehr schnell, weil wir da viel zu lange gewartet haben, denn ich will, das zeigen die Bilder in der Ausstellung ja auch, nicht in ein paar Jahren an denselben Stellen stehen, an denen ich jetzt noch Wald photographiert habe und dann ist da nur noch eine Wüste.

*Katrin Schubert:* Die Ausstellung ist also auch ein Beitrag zu einem Bewusstseinswandel, dass wir anders leben müssen, wenn wir überleben wollen in einer von ökologischen und ökonomischen Katastrophen bedrohten Welt?

*Michael Holst:* Also für mich ist die ganze Kunst das. Weil: Kunst ist meine Art in der Welt zu sein und auf mein in der Welt sein zu reagieren. Ich finde auch, dass das die Aufgabe von Kunst ist. Aber es ist nur ein kleiner Schritt. Da kann man natürlich sagen, dass ganz viele kleine Schritte auch einen großen Schritt erzeugen. Doch ich kann da nicht mehr so optimistisch sein. Wir haben als Menschen, so als Menschheit insgesamt, viel zu lange gar nichts, oder einfach das Falsche gemacht. Manchmal habe ich auch ein schlechtes Gewissen, wenn ich da die gestorbenen Wälder ästhetisch photographiere.

In der Romantik hat man ja auch den Verfall, also zum Beispiel künstliche Ruinen in einer Gartenlandschaft, ästhetisch inszeniert. Also das ist ein schwieriges Thema, aber eines dem man nicht ausweichen darf. Und ja, es ist meine Art damit umzugehen. Aber ich will das nicht zu sehr in den Vordergrund stellen, hier in dem Gespräch, denn ich denke Kunst soll, kann und muss auch aus sich selbst heraus wirken, so ohne Erklärung, so wie es auch in dieser Ausstellung die Schildchen nicht gibt, zu den Bildern. Und dann sind die Gedanken, die die Bilder, die die Ausstellung auslösen, bei den

Menschen, die sie besuchen, besucht haben, wichtiger als meine Gedanken. Also, da nehme ich mich jetzt ganz zurück. Da soll das Werk sprechen. Von daher meine Einladung, einfach noch einmal durch die Ausstellung gehen, die Bilder auf sich wirken lassen und es wird dann ja auch wieder einen Katalog geben, der zumindest etwas von der Ausstellung auch für diejenigen erfahrbar macht, die die Ausstellung nicht besuchen konnten. Und diese Erfahrung, die jeder machen kann, mit meinen Bildern, das ist meine Antwort.

*Katrin Schubert:* Ich denke, die Einladung einfach noch einmal in die Ausstellung zu gehen, sie ist ja heute noch bis 21 Uhr geöffnet, ist ein gutes Wort zum Abschluss. Vielen Dank.

# **_LANDSCAPE**

## **_ "actually everything is landscape"**

*Transcript of the panel discussion Katrin Schubert had
with Michael Holst at the finissage of the exhibition
"LANDSCAPE" on October 11, 2021.*

*Katrin Schubert:* Let me start with a provocation, even if
you might say that the artist is responsible for the provocation *(smiles)*. I'll just try to swap roles for once: Landscape, well, if I hadn't seen the exhibition, the fascination
of these wonderful pictures, which sometimes have an
almost magical effect, perhaps also because of the way
they are presented in the rooms, well, then I probably
would have said: Landscape? What's that about? Is that a
current topic today: landscape photography?

*Michael Holst:* I think that's a good question and not at all
provocative *(laughs)*. In terms of art history, landscape
or landscape painting, landscape photography, is a very
classical subject. And classical subjects are important,
that's why they are classical subjects. I'm not at all afraid
to face that. And then it's just a very diverse subject.
What is around us is landscape. Actually, everything is
landscape, you could say, even if that's wrong, of course,
or simply a nonsensical definition. But it's always a question, for example, whether it's landscape, what I'm photographing there, or whether it's the portrait of a tree, for
example, standing there in the landscape.

*Katrin Schubert:* Yes, okay, I understand that. But there are many classic subjects, so once again my question: why landscape?

*Michael Holst:* Well, if you want a very personal answer, then simply because I am in it and because it inspires me. Also because I deal with it, have to deal with it, and also want to deal with it, and that's what I do with photography, with painting, too, of course, but in this exhibition, in this project, I do it with photography.

*Katrin Schubert:* There are also drawings by you in the exhibition, even if they don't strike you as drawings at first glance.

*Michael Holst:* You mean the design of the walls.

*Katrin Schubert:* Yes. Sometimes it looks — excuse me for saying so — like scratches or impurities, these black lines that at first can't be assigned at all.

*Michael Holst:* Yes. But it's nice that you identified these lines as drawings. And they are indeed drawings. — As a child, even as a very small child, I always liked to rummage through my parents' bookcases. — Curiosity is, after all, something very important, and I would encourage everyone to keep it. — We had a big bookcase in the living room, so classically made of oak, and in the lower part of the bookcase there were doors in front of the compartments, which I could easily open as a child. And there were all books, mostly larger and heavier books, illustrated books, for example. My parents had put them there because they were standing on the base of the bookcase and couldn't bend the shelves. Heavy books can also bend quite stable shelves and the shelves of cabinets. And there was also a illustrated book about Stone Age caves, about the caves inhabited by the first humans, and there were also these wonderful cave paintings. Partly as large-format color photographs, but also as drawings. I think they were drawings, black and white line drawings that the archaeologists had made for documentation. And these drawings are very abstract. And that appealed to me as a child. And on the inside pages of the book cover there were also some lines of these drawings, simply as a graphic motif, some lines, quite roughly and in red on the white paper with which the inside of the book cover was lined at the front and back.

Much later, when I was already in high school, my mother once leafed through the book one evening and said to me when I came into the room, "Look, this is one of the books you used to draw in when you were a child." And I was quite amazed, because I was sure that those drawings there were not mine. And I looked closely at the pages and that was printed. You could see well the raster of the print. But my mother didn't believe it, even when I showed her the raster of the print with a magnifying glass, she didn't believe it. She was quite sure that these lines were mine. Since then I have always drawn such lines from time to time, not in books and not on walls, as it is actually with the cave painting, but whole notebooks have been filled it. I like these little notebooks that I always carry around with me and in which I always quickly draw something when something occurs to me.

And when I was thinking about how to design the walls for the exhibition concept, which we built into the exhibition rooms in order to be able to place all the pictures, it occurred to me — after the team had already left, and I took another look at everything, so that I knew how far we had come and what still had to be done the following day — that I somehow had the idea that I thought, this is now your chance, here you have so many wonderful walls on which you can draw these lines. The cave paintings are also landscape paintings, animals in a landscape, partly also sky and stars. Some can even be assigned to a very specific date, a specific astronomical constellation. That is really exciting. And now, as I stood in the shell of the freshly painted exhibition walls, there was this great impulse in me to insert lines, these lines of landscapes, where one line tells the story of an entire landscape, as the cave paintings do, and then I really started to draw these lines on the freshly painted walls. And that was an act of genesis and that also had something liberating and something of coming home, of arriving after a long time or journey. And at first I just did it for myself, thinking, tomorrow you'll take a bucket of paint and paint over the whole thing again, and when the painters come, in the afternoon, to continue their work — we had a very tight schedule in setting up the exhibition — then it will all be forgotten again, wiped off, painted over. It was just for me. But then I left it, and that's how these lines got into the exhibition.

*Katrin Schubert:* The presentation is quite unconventional. In any case, it's striking. I've read a whole series of reviews that criticize the lack of any description in the exhibition. There are no texts explaining the exhibition, not even a label for the pictures, that little sign that you find in every museum, in every exhibition, usually at the bottom right, next to the picture or the exhibit. And maybe that doesn't say much if there's a name and a work title, but ...

*Michael Holst:* ... you say that yourself, that doesn't say much, such a title. Although that doesn't has to be true at all, there are also works that couldn't exist without the title. Marcel Duchamp's objet trouvé, for example, this work of art only comes into being by making it a work of art, by naming it a work of art, by giving it a name.

But to the landscapes and why the pictures here have no titles and therefore also not these little labels. That's the way it is with landscape: Today, every point on earth has a name, at least a number, that is, the combination of latitude and longitude, and most places also have a name, usually even many and very different ones, which they have received in the course of history, from the people who have lived there or who have traveled there. And then there is also a whole set of names for the different landscapes in each language: meadow, steppe, desert, mountains and so on, and in landscape painting there are types of landscapes that have developed in the course of art history, and there are artists who play with these motifs, vary them, caricature them or simply imitate them. This is, historically, art-historically, and also simply linguistically — just take place names — a huge conglomeration of designations, of words, ultimately of letters and numbers, with which we humans have covered or infused our world. And digitization, simply because it's technically possible, has then taken it to the extreme. There is a very high-resolution model of the surface of the earth. I can look at an aerial photograph of practically any place, in great detail, simply by scrolling through the surface of a search engine provider's website. And that tells me: There is nothing left to discover on this planet. Everything has already been photographed and mapped and recorded. As an artist, I stand against this. We need a new view. That's what art is all about. And with this landscape project, I simply wanted to free the landscape from all this ballast, to get rid of all that, to simply give the landscape the opportunity to be as it is, in its appearance in which it meets me when I stand in it. The landscape does not need the names we have given it.

*Katrin Schubert:* But now, when I see a picture in the exhibition, I don't know where it is, what it shows, and I don't know when it was taken. I don't know which river is flowing through the landscape or what the name of the mountain is on whose hilltops I see cut-down trees.

*Michael Holst:* Yes, and that's how it should be, because that's also how it is when I stand in the landscape, the way I stand in the landscape as an artist, or the way I think an artist should stand in the landscape, namely unprejudiced, and unprejudiced also means without prior knowledge. And if you look at it from a very fundamental point of view, then you can't know, or don't know at all, what this mountain or the river, to stay with the examples you mentioned, really is, according to its essence, according to its inner being.

There is a very prominent mountain in the Andes — I'm now not saying the name we have given it today — that the indigenous people, who are called Indians in our language, which is curious because they were never in India, but because someone who wanted to explore — actually take possession of — the land where their ancestors lived, thought he was in India — that these indigenous people, probably the first people to encounter this mountain, who may have climbed it, or always seen it from a distance because it's so recognizable in the landscape, that they gave it a name. A few syllables, consonants and vowels, in a combination that for a European living today cannot be pronounced without stumbling. And of course the question arises: What is the right name now? A name only works if I associate something with it. And if I am unprejudiced, really unprejudiced, then things have no name. I don't know anything about them. They are just there. And the beauty of photography is that you can — at least I try to — capture such an unprejudiced impression with the camera. A view of so many possible views, but just a view of a thing, a something, in this case just a landscape. And that's why there are no titles, next to or under the pictures, that's why there are no words, because everything that the picture — this one impression — says is in the picture. Complete. There is no need for a title.

*Katrin Schubert:* I went through the exhibition once last week and watched the visitors, listened to them. And I noticed that when they talked about the pictures, they gave them names: "The Meadow Picture", or "The Night Tower", for example. And my question now is: Doesn't that show that the concept with the missing names doesn't work, that it can't work?

*Michael Holst (laughs):* No, quite the opposite. That is something wonderful that you have observed. People are in the exhibition, they see an image, they have an experience and then they talk to each other about it. Man is a being that is designed for communication. No one can be alone. And then they realize that they need names for this communication, to talk about what they see, what they have seen, their experience, their sensory impression. And then they spontaneously create these labels for themselves, which are not there, just as the impression of the picture creates it for them. And I think it's great that you made this observation, even on a normal exhibition day and not just at the opening, where everything was full and people came to talk to each other. And the example you gave, "Nachtturm" (Night Tower), that's a great title for a picture, it's just wonderful what happens with the visitors. And it works, I think, for everyone who goes through the exhibition. The visitors search, make their own labels, or however you want to put it. If they were to take out an atlas now to refer to a certain place on their map, a place, based on the topography that the picture shows, and then said: "Oh yes, that's the Allalin glacier, and it's probably a picture from the 1970s, because it's still completely covered with snow and it actually looks nicer if you take a picture of it from a slightly more northerly point", then something would have gone wrong in the exhibition, because then the impression would no longer appear as it is, the picture would no longer be an image, but a sign for something that is assigned to the sign. The picture becomes a sign and that is exactly what I don't want in this exhibition.

*Katrin Schubert:* How do you deal with criticism? It's not always positive either.

*Michael Holst:* Well, I don't have a problem with that at all. Quite the opposite. So now, for instance, in relation to this project: a critic, I actually can't remember who it was *(laughs)*, — that's also one of my ways of dealing with it — there was a very specific review of this exhibition that said that the landscapes in this project were the most stereotypical thing he had seen from me so far. Somehow that's how he put it, and I don't think he meant it in a negative way, even if it's not right, but I understand how he comes to that, because many — not all — of the pictures in the exhibition are made with an extreme wide-angle, not fisheye, but 35 mm, 24 mm, mostly really the 24 mm. And it's always a similar position of the viewer, even though I was of course always standing in a completely different place, in a completely different landscape, when I took the pictures. I think that's simply my view of landscape, as shaped by this project. And then I think it's okay if a critic writes it that way. Of course, it annoys my dealer when there is something there that can be understood negatively. "Stereotype" is not positive in itself when you say it about art. And today, with the electronic media, everything is very sensitive. Individual sentences are passed on in isolation and then suddenly something becomes a problem that wasn't a problem at all or wasn't criticism. But for me that's okay. I always try to understand how someone comes to such an opinion or view and then it clears up, mostly.

*Katrin Schubert:* I also read in a review that what you are showing is not landscape at all.

*Michael Holst:* Well, I already said something about it, that it is not so easy to say or determine where landscape begins and where landscape ends, or what landscape is. And of course I photograph the tree standing there in the landscape and the forest. And I also think that the village, the town or the city that are in the landscape are part of the landscape. Whereby that is already a contrast, city and country. — And that's still a setting: landscape equals countryside. — And if I say, as I did at the beginning of our conversation, that everything is landscape, then of course that doesn't make any sense from a definitional point of view, but it does from an artistic point of view. That's the beauty of art, that it can also do contradictory things. When I look at a city, I can also look at it as a landscape; as a designed landscape, as a redesigned landscape, perhaps also as an occupied landscape, perhaps also as a destroyed landscape. It all depends on the view. And I have different views when I take photographs. The important thing as an artist is to be aware of this view and to make others aware of it.

*Katrin Schubert:* Is that then what makes the photographs of an artist different from the photos I take as a non-professional with the camera of my mobile phone?

*Michael Holst:* Oh, I wouldn't say that at all. I actually can't remember who said that everyone is an artist, I think it was Andy Warhol who said that, and it was Beuys who said that with the potato peeling. So I really think that everyone is an artist, according to possibility in any case, and especially today, when we have so many technical possibilities to make and process images, more and more people can also develop abilities to let the artist they are become active. And I think it's really stupid, I'll put it that way, when people say that the mobile phone is replacing the camera and that there are now countless bad images, more bad images than ever before, and that no one can take proper photographs any more. No, that's not right.

I can buy a really good professional camera for really not much money already, and the cameras in mobile phones are also getting technically better and better. That's fascinating. And of course there are countless bad images, lacking in imagination, technically terrible and without any inspiration, but there are also countless fascinatingly good images, full of new ideas, views, perspectives, you just have to see them in the great stream of images that we create. And that is exactly what art is. And when someone leaves my exhibition, takes out his mobile phone and takes a picture of exactly what he sees there, then perhaps he does it a little bit differently than he would have done otherwise, before visiting the

192

exhibition, and perhaps in the evening, when he wants to send one of the photos to a friend — that is also the fascinating thing, that we can send these photos to any place in the world — then maybe he chooses a picture that is different from the pictures he usually sends and the picture has, because of the changed view, taken on a quality that it didn't have otherwise, and that's where the artist has become active.

And my wish is that people keep this, that they cultivate it, these many small changes in the view and their ability to become aware of it, and to let it become visible, for example in a mobile phone photo, and maybe one day I will buy a compact camera or a mirrorless system camera with a good lens. And then I develop my skills there. Or I take a pencil, which is also a reaction, and start drawing the lines that I see in the picture, that I see in my surroundings, and then art begins, and I would like to invite all visitors of the exhibition to do that. I don't claim to be the better artist. Art is not elitist, everyone can make art and I think everyone should do so.

*Katrin Schubert:* What role does time play for you when you photograph landscape?

*Michael Holst:* Landscape is time. That is my experience. Landscape changes continuously, always, and this change takes place at very different speeds. Especially with light and wind, landscape experiences enormous speeds. There is such a notion that landscape is something static, long exposure times and so on. But for me this is not true. I may see a subject, and in the short time it takes me to get my camera out — I'm actually quite fast — everything has already changed.

But there are also the slow changes. Sometimes I come to a place where I took a photo one, two, or even three years ago. There are certain images that accompany me. They are in me, even when I am in completely different places. And then it happens that I simply have a longing for this place, as it is in my memory. I want to go there again, to see it once more, to feel the air, perhaps the characteristic smell and the look. And then — I almost want to say naturally — everything is different or many things. It can be small changes, seasons, weather, time of day, but it can also be radical changes. The forest is gone. There is only a cleared slope, the ground rutted by monstrously rough tires. Currently, this is very often the case, especially where there was spruce. And then you have to take a look, take a breath. There is then sadness, but also, with me it works like that when I have the camera in my hand, that's a help for me, because it's a tool that tells me: do something with me, use me, you have a job. And then I make something out of it. So just in the last two years, a lot of landscape pictures have been taken. Many sad ones, too. I don't want to deny that. And there we are again with time, that was your question. One of the essential characteristics of time is that it passes. If it did not pass, there would be no time. Without passing, there is no time. And when I take pictures out of time with the camera, which are also in time again, they also age, the digital pictures much more slowly than the analog ones, so in general. But digital images can also age quite radically, if there is a loss of data, they age so extremely from one moment to the next that they are no longer there. It's all very fragile, our digital electrical way of recording.

In museums, there is this discourse among art historians, and especially among conservators and restorers, about how far one should or may intervene in the aging process of a work of art. What about the patina, for example, is one such question. My photographs are all digital. They're not going to get a patina. Maybe at some point you can't read some files completely and some pixels are white or magenta or some parts of the image have black streaks. But most likely, at some point they will simply not be readable at all because the media is broken or the software no longer exists with which to view the images on a monitor or imagesetter. The exposed image, for example, the set of exposed images that I have now created for the exhibition and the copies that come into the gallery for sale, they exist now and they age, just as the chemical processes of the materials from which they are made cause them to age. You choose materials that are very resistant to aging, light, and so on, and it's quite amazing what quality a professional photo paper can have today, for example, or an ink print. But that also ages, of course, and I think it should. Yes, you can and should resist changes, especially those that are not good; but you also have to accept change. It's really a difficult balance. And my attempt to find this balance between rebelling, revolting, contradicting and simply accepting, that's what I try to do in my pictures. They are for me something like a measure, a line that gives me support in this oscillation of time.

*Katrin Schubert:* What surprised me was the, shall I say, very unconventional hanging. I mean especially the, let me put it this way, uneven presentation of the paintings across the exhibition space. In the large hall, the largest room of the exhibition area, there is only one picture. With its four meters thirty by almost two meters ninety — I looked it up once again — it is indeed really large. But it doesn't fill the room. There would be plenty of room for more pictures. Other rooms are very tightly hung, there are partitions built in, almost a labyrinth. In the second room, for example, which is much smaller, there are ten pictures, also large formats. Why is this so?

*Michael Holst:* I think that has something to do with rhythm. When we developed the concept for the hanging, I really started with Hall 1. And the pictures were exposed especially for the exhibition. So we didn't know the exact size yet, at least not for all the pictures. We first looked at the floor plans, and the team also had the idea of simply achieving a distribution as even as possible, so that each image has the space it needs to be viewed. And that would also have been a good concept, simply to make it possible to experience the story that these images tell in their sequence, in their interrelatedness.

But when I was in the rooms for the first time — it was actually the great hall that was the first room I was in — I knew I wanted to have one really big picture here in this huge space and only one and I didn't want it to seem big. I want everybody to wonder where the other pictures are, and so from that point of view, I think your question is a good one. It shows me that the concept worked. — The picture is big, and that's how it looked to you, but the room is bigger. And that's a statement. It's landscape, which is the focus of the exhibition. And this really large landscape image hangs in a room that is larger than the image, that makes a more voluminous, I don't want to say more powerful, impression than the landscape. That is our relationship to landscape, today. We have taken it over, placed it in the space of our gripping understanding. But with that, in fact, we have understood nothing.

And now to the other rooms. They are all designed very differently. I also received feedback from a visitor that she thought she had been to completely different exhibitions in this one exhibition. Simply because each room is so individually designed, or rather, the pictures are always hung according to completely different concepts. And that's the thing about rhythm. An exhibition has to pulsate. And I don't have a prescribed or recommended tour here, as it is the case in many of my other exhibitions. This time we deliberately designed it freely, and the architecture allows that. I can get from any room to any other, almost always directly, sometimes with a small detour through a corridor, a gallery or a staircase, where there are also a few pictures hanging that lead me over or perhaps distract me. And if I then, for example, one possibility, come from the large Hall 1 into Hall 4 — which is much smaller —, there are then over 50 pictures hanging. I almost said small pictures, but that's not right at all, they are usually at least 60 by 60 cm, and the panoramas are sometimes one meter thirty or wider. And they hang in such a way that you always have enough space to look at them properly. The built-in walls have created many intimate rooms, show rooms, with individual light, just as each picture requires. The idea was that you can see a lot very quickly without having to walk a long way.

There are these rooms with standard light that are used to develop digital images or to filter them out for prepress, for example. We practically built a room around each image, the space that a person needs to be able to view this image optimally and in a relaxed, inspiring atmosphere. There's also always comfortable seating, all individually designed. We did a lot for that.

It was a real challenge, and the team did a great job. You can try it out for yourself: Just walk slowly through the rooms that have been built into this hall for the exhibition, I would almost say these rooms are grown into it, they are organically distributed, and then you will notice that you can feel the rhythm of the hanging. And if you come from the large Hall 1, which we have allowed to retain its voluminousness, then you will notice here, in the compression, that you as a visitor have the capacity to absorb this density. You see a lot and you see intensively and richly varied and it is not an overload. On the contrary, there is a calm.

*Katrin Schubert:* Speaking of the pictures in Hall 4. Maybe you could say something about the Duals. I think they don't explain themselves on their own.

*Michael Holst:* Oh, maybe they do, they should, at least the pictures. With the term, Duals, that's where it's a little bit different. I understand that. But that's okay, too. Duals (Duale) is a term or a word that I took from Paul Julius Kleiber. And first of all, it has nothing to do with landscape and nothing to do with photography. As a draftsman, which is what I am also, I for a while studied Paul Julius Kleiber very intensively. He developed — there is a wonderful linguistic essay by Michale Antenberg — his own terminology for his drawings. When he draws tangles of intertwining lines on a sheet of paper and then creates two of these structures next to each other, he calls them Duals. These are drawings, after all, on a sheet of paper or cardboard. If you would make a classical painting out of it, in a format of one-twenty by one-twenty, for example, a typical measurement for an exhibition, and then hang two of these square canvases next to each other, then you would simply call it a dyptichon. And for me it was like this now, that when I developed this concept of the landscape parts relating to each other, or also landscape parts deriving from each other or out of each other, I had to think of Kleiber's Duals and there I simply took the liberty of taking his term here.

*Katrin Schubert:* Most Duals are square or almost square, and there is usually a repetition. This is not always obvious at first glance, but usually parts that can be seen in one picture can also be found in the other.

*Michael Holst:* I have to be a little bit careful now, so as not to encourage any misunderstandings. To be on the safe side, the Duals are not stereo images, nor are they intended to be. But a special kind of stereo photography was an inspiration for me for this kind of image presentation. Stereophotography is a very old technique. Two pictures are taken of the same object, usually with two cameras at the same time, from a position that is offset exactly by the distance between the eyes. And there are these wonderful cards on which two square images, just these two shots, are exposed side by side and you can then look at them with special glasses into which the card is inserted. And I once saw a whole collection of such cards at a photographer friend's house, from the early days of photography, on this old photographic paper that gets its wonderful coloring from the silver oxide, but which is still very stable today. And since then, I always find such a presentation of two square images side by side very interesting, even if they are not stereo photographs.

Now actually, the square is really not the classic format for landscape presentations. Landscape is oblong. You can print a city panorama on a ruler and sell it to tourists as a souvenir. The longer the better. If I now hang two squares next to each other, then in a sense I'm taking back the width. Maybe there are just two square windows next to each other and I look through them into or onto the landscape. With some of the Duals, that's really the case. They are simply two square sections of a landscape image. There's no repetition there then at all.

With many of the Duals, however, I also did it in such a way that I simply put a square on the left part of a picture and then, of course, something of the landscape is missing there on the right, and for the second Dual I then simply put the square on the left of the picture and something is missing on the right, but on both cutouts there is something of the middle part of the picture together. And that has, just with the repetition you noted, something relaxing, calming. Somehow the pictures also become more formal when they hang next to each other like this. There is also, and this is especially important for the gallery, always a scale with the distance at which the two pictures should hang from each other. And, that's also one of the things that was difficult for my gallerist at first: you can only ever buy both duals together. That was important to me. You can't tear these images apart. My gallery owner said that this was something that had to be explained to the customer. But I think that's okay, and I also have the impression that the prospective buyers understand that.

*Katrin Schubert:* Today it is the case in practically every museum, in every art exhibition, that taking photographs is prohibited. Here with you, at this exhibition, it's different. Why?

*Michael Holst: (laughs)* Well, there's a very simple reason for that: I myself like to take photos in museums and at exhibitions, fairs and so on; in places where people come to look at things. *(Seriously again.)* So you can take really wonderful photos of people who are so attentively absorbed in looking at things, who talk to each other about what they're seeing, and then you understand what's being shown in a completely different way. But of course that's not the real reason here *(laughs).* — Well, maybe it is. — I could take pictures in my own exhibition even if it were forbidden for the visitors. — But seriously: Today, practically everyone has his cell phone with him, and it usually has a great camera, we've already talked about that. And the quite natural reflex is that one, if one sees something beautiful, something which pleases one, takes out this device, which one has anyway nearly the whole time of the day in the hand, at least always ready to hand, and of what one finds there straight beautiful, interesting, important, however always, makes a photo. And why should I forbid people to do that. On the contrary. I want to encourage them to take pictures, to sharpen their eye for good, for exciting, interesting, inspired images, and it's wonderful if I start there in the exhibition.

*Katrin Schubert:* And what about copyrights? As an artist, you can't simply waive them, can you? That's a big issue, also economically and legally.

*Michael Holst:* Well, I don't do that. The fact that people are allowed to take pictures in the exhibition does not mean that they are allowed to reproduce my pictures. Yes, it's true that cameras, even the small and handy ones and also the ones in cell phones, are getting better and better. But if I want to make a real reproduction of a picture that is hanging in the exhibition, then I have to illuminate everything properly, no one is allowed to pass by or cast a shadow on it. There are always reflections that interfere. To avoid parallax distortion, I have to have the right angle. With the big pictures I would have to take a ladder to have the right position and even then: the original printed by me, the artist, is completely different than what I get when I make a print from my cell phone photo. And I think the people who are interested in art, they know that too.

And anyone who wants to take an impression of the exhibition home with him or her, who perhaps captures an interesting scene with the visitors, the way they stand in the room, the way they reflect the light and look at a picture, should do so. That's then also his work of art and I find it simply wonderful and also the sense of an exhibition that then just also my — yes copyrighted — picture is to be seen on this picture. And if this, my, picture has led to the fact that the scene in the space of the exhibition has happened in such a way, yes, that is of course what my share in the art is. But without the visitors an exhibition is nothing and without the people who look at my pictures, my pictures are not what they should be and therefore I am happy when people photograph that, they take home the picture that has arisen there with them, in the head, first, with the device, the cell phone or the compact camera, with what they just have with them.

And then there's always the issue of publication. I have nothing against that either, and that is also written at the entrance to the exhibition and at the checkroom, and there are notes where the whole thing is explained again, legally exact and I think also understandable. If I take pictures in the exhibition, make pictures just for me, then that is no problem at all, and with pleasure also occasionally a print or a printout, which I hang over my desk. And if I send one of the pictures to a friend, by email or via messenger, even to the whole group, friends, family, work colleagues and so on, then that's all okay. Even a private post on social media, that's okay. It's good for us, for the exhibition. I don't want to forbid anyone to talk about what he has experienced, what inspires him, I don't want to forbid anyone to communicate. And today for communication there are many channels and photos are a natural part of it. That's great.

Of course, there is also the problem of the personal rights of those people depicted. There is a rule that if the individual person is no longer recognizable as an individual, but rather a group of people is depicted — it is always assumed that there are seven or more people — then there is no longer a problem with personal rights. But if I depict a single person, then of course I can't do that without their consent. For this reason, we would like to point out to our visitors that they may be photographed in the exhibition and that there is a possibility that they will be depicted in the resulting pictures. At the same time, we ask visitors not to take pictures of individuals, unless of course they are friends or acquaintances who wish them to do so. By the way, there is one picture — the members of the team who are always in the exhibition told me — in front of which especially many visitors like to take a selfie. I do not say now which picture that is.

*Katrin Schubert:* And what about commercial use?

*Michael Holst:* That's not allowed, of course. If someone wants to do that, then we have to talk about a license, and that also involves costs. For this exhibition we had two requests and it was too expensive for them, which

I can't understand at all, because the price wasn't that high, but it has to be in fair proportion to the expected profit. Whoever earns money with my work should also give me a share of what he earns with what I have done. I do not work for free. I can not do that at all. As an artist, I am also an entrepreneur and I think it is also a part of making art that you can make your living with it, from it. You contribute your life time, your ideas, your energy and creativity. So for me, this is a question of justice. And I am also of the opinion that one does not have to regulate anything with prohibitions. If, for example, reproductions of my pictures were to appear that were made from photographs taken in the exhibition, then that would be noticed, and these pictures would not sell, and my dealer would take action against that. So here I have no worries at all.

*Katrin Schubert:* Finally, perhaps one more critical question. I have heard from some exhibition visitors that they miss something in the exhibition. Or that they had expected something else in addition. I mean, the visitors were all very enthusiastic, that's true, and you could see that in the exhibition. The atmosphere was really great on all days and in many cases electrifying, that's what one visitor said when I talked to him about his experience. But just because of that, there was also something missing. Some visitors also asked whether this was perhaps even intended and whether the exhibition, also in the tension to its title, landscape, has created a break there, perhaps also intended: There are no deserts and no glaciers, the exotic is missing. Africa, America, Australia, Asia. Entire continents are missing. Why?

*Michael Holst:* Yes, that is a very important question. And I've been asked that quite a few times, too. It wasn't the most frequent question, but one that I was often asked. And yes, when I hear the title "Landscape" as the title for an exhibition of photographs, then of course the expectation comes to me of the exotic, of deserts, for example, great dune panoramas of the Sahara, where the sun makes the sand glow and where I think I can still feel this glow when I look at the picture. Or I think of a picture in which, in a, let's say, already deeply dark sky above a steppe already almost completely swallowed by twilight, a single star glitters into the viewer's eyes. Or the fascinating rock formations of the Grand Canyon into which I fall with the camera and stage this fall in such a way in a large-format picture that the viewer still feels the pressure in the stomach area, which I as a photographer must have had, when I made these pictures.

Yes, I think there are thousands of examples of images that arise as an expectation when the words "landscape" and "photography" come together. But this is now art what I do here, not travelogue. And traveling, as we do it today, I am also very self-critical here, has something colonial about it. The exotic only becomes exotic because we see it as exotic , visit it as exotic, with our journey. So, in the best case as an educational trip, in the worst case as a conquest. And our travels do have something conquering too. And for this exhibition, I wanted — this is therefore a very important, a very good question, to conclude —, for this exhibition, I wanted that — I was aware of the expectation that the title creates — I wanted that when you go into the exhibition with this — I'll put it this way now — sensational view, that you then encounter something that you can see in this way, or rather, that I see in this way, in my everyday life, in the world in which I live.

And then, of course, I have to say something about my traveling now. I think that's unavoidable when you make an exhibition with the title "Landscape": I have traveled a lot for a very long time, as we privileged Europeans and North Americans do. And of course that's a lot of air travel, and I've also done a lot of projects in Asia, some in Africa, especially South Africa, and then America. And if you take a look at the kilometers you cover and the time you need, then it's quite clear that you're using enormous resources.

Once you look at the resources, it's simply outrageous, if you convert the effort, for example, into the power that people can generate with their muscles. I don't know how many people would have to turn a dynamo with a handle for an hour to generate enough electricity to drive a car for an hour, for example at 50 kilometers per hour. And across the Atlantic, you need one or two weeks if you do it with a sailing ship, and you are already using the power of the wind. And if you do it with a kayak, really just the muscle power, then it takes just under a hundred days, so a little more than three months. And there you move only a small boat and your body and we hunt today in eight hours or even less over this distance, with a machine that weighs about 40 tons.

If you convert that, how many people would have to row for that. That's unbelievable and there we humans, the privileged part of us, we take a really unbelievable piece of resource and we take it in a way that we will never get it back. We destroy. And I just realized that in its very deep core it has something to do with attitude, with the way we look at life, at our life here on this little vulnerable planet. And that's why I decided for me to change that. Simply for me, in my life. And such a decision has an impact on what I do as an artist. I no longer get on a plane, and for this exhibition, for example, I have only chosen pictures that I have made in places that I have reached with my own muscle power, on foot, I am an enthusiastic hiker, and by bike, I have really learned to love that. Yes, I have the studio in Frankfurt, and the studio in Cologne, now yes for a few years, and that's just for me also a really great opportunity when someone says: Hey I want you to come to Cologne, have good working conditions in the city and make art here. And then of course I travel between the two locations. But I try to organize it in such a way that I reduce the number of trips, that I don't go back and forth two or three times a week like I used to, but maybe only once or twice a month, and then always by train and no longer by plane, which is completely nonsensical now, when I can get from Frankfurt to Cologne by train in 50 minutes, because in that time I haven't even checked in on the plane, so it's a bit exaggerated, but sometimes it can be that way. From that point of view, it has changed my life a lot and with it, it has changed my art.

And the change still goes on. And there you can also use technology, positively. For example, I have many customers in Asia, collectors who are interested in my pictures, and some of them even have the ambition, for example, to have a print of every photograph that I show in an exhibition that is numbered with two digits, that is, a maximum of number 99 of a picture. And in the past I used to print the pictures at my place, sign them and send them out. Now we have found a way to sign the pictures digitally. And that is accepted by the people who collect art, and so now I have a service provider on site who prints the pictures and then the collector can pick up the picture there and through the network that we can use there, there is the guarantee that the distance for the shipment is never more than 230 km. — So that's 200 miles, the Americans still like to calculate in miles, and that's why the 230 km. — And I think that's already a small step, and we need many of these small steps so that it becomes a big step, and I think we need it, and we need it very quickly, because we've waited far too long, because I don't want to be standing in a few years, as the pictures in the exhibition also show, in the same places where I've photographed forests now, and then there's only a desert.

*Katrin Schubert:* So the exhibition is also a contribution to a change in awareness that we have to live differently if we want to survive in a world threatened by ecological and economic catastrophes?

*Michael Holst:* So for me, all art is that. Because art is my way of being in the world and reacting to my being in the world. I also think that's the task of art. But it's only a small step. Of course you can say that many small steps also create a big step. But I can no longer be so optimistic. As human beings, as humanity as a whole, we have done nothing for far too long, or simply done the wrong thing. Sometimes I also have a guilty conscience when I photograph the dead forests aesthetically.

In Romanticism, decay was also staged aesthetically, for example, artificial ruins in a garden landscape. So that's a difficult subject, but one that you can't avoid. And yes, it is my way of dealing with it. But I don't want to put that too much in the foreground, here in the conversation, because I think art should, can and must also work out of itself, so without explanation, just as there are no labels for the pictures in this exhibition. And then the thoughts that the pictures, which the exhibition triggers, in the people who visit it, have visited, are more important than my thoughts. So, there I now take myself back completely. Let the work speak. So my invitation is simply to go through the exhibition again, let the pictures have an effect on you, and then there will also be a catalog, which will at least allow those who were unable to visit the exhibition to experience something of the exhibition. And this experience that everyone can make, with my pictures, that is my answer.

*Katrin Schubert:* I think the invitation simply to go to the exhibition again, it is still open today until 9 p.m., is a good word to conclude with. Thank you very much.

# Quellenangaben | Sources

**Neue Waschbeckenbilder | New washbasin pictures**
Sandra Farinelli im Gespräch mit Michael Holst am 09.04.2025 im Forum72 Basel. Transkription Andrea Wassmanshausen und Claudia Tom. Redaktion Kathrin Schubert. Englische Fassung Ugur Tomson. Erstveröffentlichung mit freundlicher Genehmigung der Gesprächspartner. First publication with kind permission of the interviewees.


**the invisible | un-sichtbar**
Texte aus | Quotations: Holst, Michael; Menke, Marcellus M. (2025): The Invisible digital images Michael Holst. 2. Auflage. conTEMPart-Edition, Cologne. ISBN 9783819051678


**142.129 Wäscheständer in der Wüste |
142,129 drying racks in a desert**

Texte aus | Quotations: Holst, Michael; Menke, Marcellus M. (2019): 142.129 Wäscheständer in der Wüste von Nevada Projekt einer Installation für Christo und Jeanne-Claude. conTEMPart-Edition, Cologne. ISBN 9783750463530

**flusen |fluffs**

Texte aus | Quotations: Holst, Michael; Menke, Marcellus M. (2020): Flusen | Fluffs Geschichte einer Installation | Story of an installation. conTEMPart-Edition, Cologne. ISBN 9783751933070


**LANDSCHAFT | LANDSCAPE**

Texte aus | Quotations: Holst, Michael; Menke, Marcellus M. (2021): LANDSCHAFT photographien Michael Holst. 1. Auflage. conTEMPart-Edition, Cologne. ISBN 9783755755715

**MICHAEL HOLST** conTEMPart-Edition

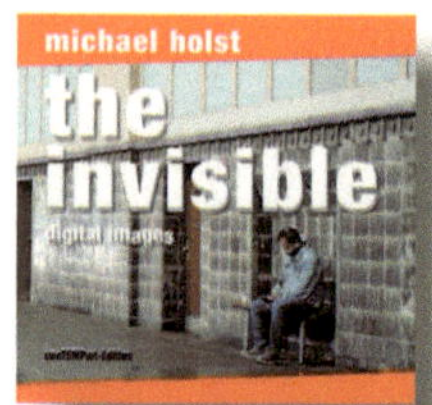


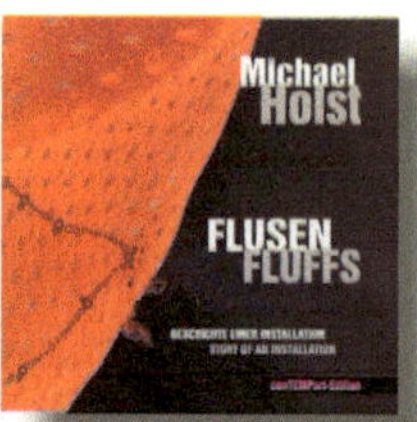


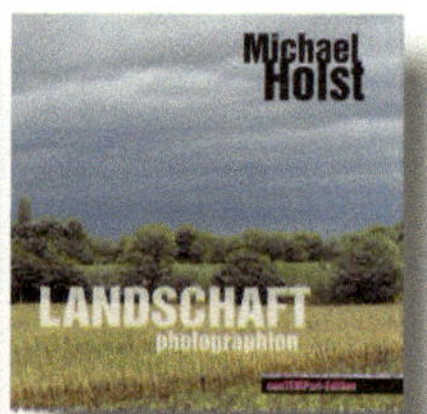


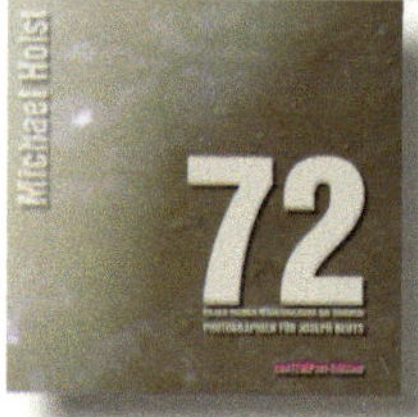


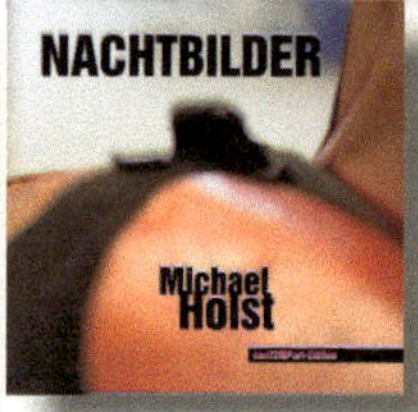

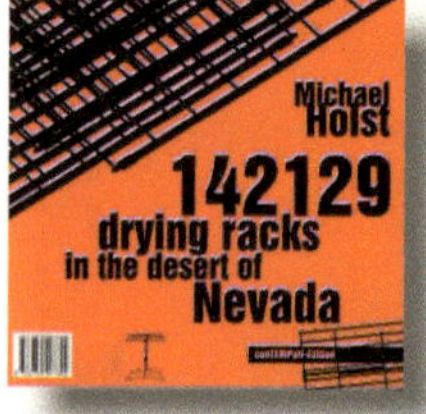


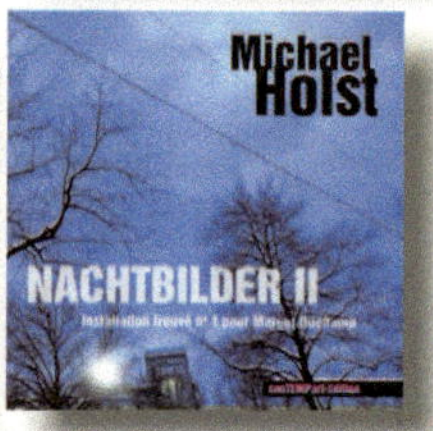


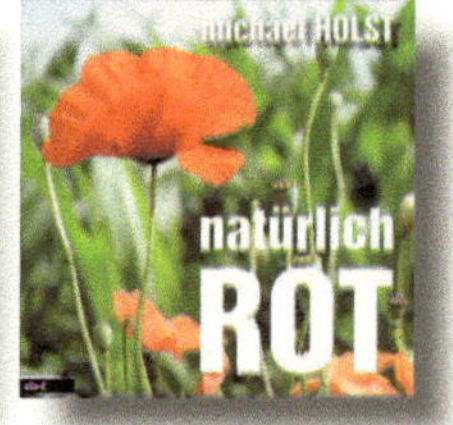


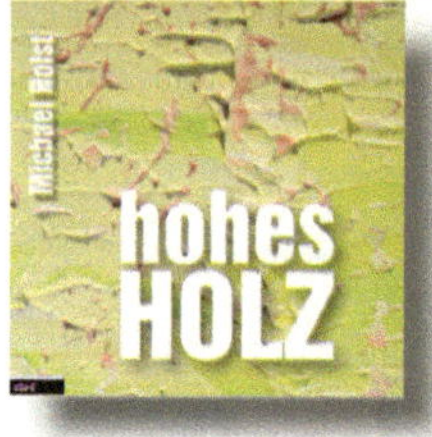


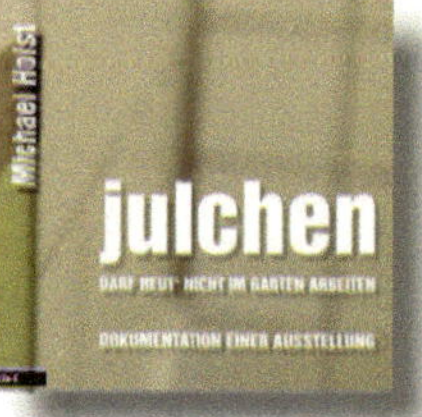


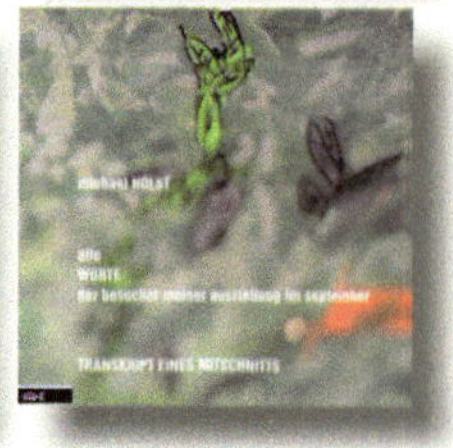


# Michael Holst

conTEMPart-Edition

„72 Bilder meines
Waschbeckens
am Morgen"
ISBN 9783752822458

„Nachtbilder"
ISBN 9783748120193

„142129
Wäscheständer
in der Wüste von
Nevada"
ISBN 9783750407824

„Nachtbilder II"
ISBN 9783750486898

„Flusen | Fluffs"
ISBN 9783751933070

„Landschaft"
ISBN 9783755755715

„The Invisible.
Digital Images"
ISBN 9783819051678

# MICHAEL HOLST contEMPart-Edition

Der Künstler Michael Holst ist ein wahrhaftiger Universalist. Er arbeitet mit den unterschiedlichsten Medien und Techniken. Sein Werk umfasst sowohl ganz klassische Arbeiten auf Leinwand und Papier, aber auch Skulpturen und umfangreiche Installationen. Ein von ihm geschätztes Medium ist die digitale Photographie. Er erstellt mit ihr beeindruckende Prints in den unterschiedlichsten Formaten und er dokumentiert mit ihr seine Installationen und Projektkonzepte. Diese Dokumentationen sind die Grundlage für die Bildbände der contempART-Edition. Im Band „Hohes Holz" dokumentiert er die großformatigen Ölbilder der gleichnamigen Ausstellung. Im Band „Julchen kann heut' nicht im Garten arbeiten" findet sich die Dokumentation eines Installationszyklus in einer deutschen Kleingartenkolonie. Der Band „72 Bilder meines Waschbeckens am Morgen" setzt sich mit Themen aus dem Werk von Joseph Beuys auseinander. In der Dokumentation „Nachtbilder" zeigt er Details seiner „Installation ohne Hase", in der er sich mit Motiven aus den Werken von Ewald Mataré, Joseph Beuys und Günther Uecker auseinandersetzt. „Nachtbilder II" dokumentiert die Photographien der „Installation trouvé no 1 pour Marcel Duchamp". Im Band „142129 Wäscheständer in der Wüste von Nevada" dokumentiert er die Projektkonzeption seiner Christo und Jeanne-Claude gewidmeten Installation in der Wüste von Nevada. In „Flusen | Fluffs" erzähl er die Geschichte seiner in Boston realisierten Installation mit diesen kleinen, fast nicht sichtbaren Objekte und zeigt eine Auswahl der mehr als 140.000 Photographien die das Projekt dokumentieren. Der Band "Landschaft" dokumentiert die aktuellen Landschaftsphotographien von Michael Holst aus dem Jahr 2021. Mit „the invisible" (2025) zeigt Michael Holst in seinen Bildern Dinge und deren Wesenheiten, die sich der Sichtbarkeit entziehen.

Edition HIC<